Halt in Woodbridge

Halt In Woodbridge is © 2015 Peter Robbins.
All rights reserved. No part of this book may be used or reproduced in any manner whatsoever without written permission except in the case of brief quotations in critical articles or reviews.

Robbins, Peter.
Halt in Woodbridge: An Air Force Colonel's Thirty-Year Fight To Silence An Authentic UFO Whistle-Blower / by Peter Robbins.

178 p.
ISBN 978-1517447212
1. Unidentified Flying Objects
2. History—United States—Armed Forces

First published in the United States by Peter Robbins

Cover design by Lou Ann Robinson
Cover photo © 2015 Peter Robbins

All photographs and illustrations in this book were reproduced with the kind permission of their owners, or else are in the public domain.

Manufactured in the United States of America

Halt in Woodbridge:

An Air Force Colonel's Thirty-Year Fight To Silence An Authentic UFO Whistle-Blower

By Peter Robbins

Also by Peter Robbins:

Left at East Gate: A First-Hand Account of the Rendlesham Forest UFO Incident, Its Cover-Up and Investigation. (with Larry Warren)

Deliberate Deception: A Case of Disinformation in the UFO Research Community

This book is dedicated to Dennis Patrick Warren

"Life is a storm young friend......one moment you're basking in the sunlight, the next your shattered on the rocks. What makes you a man is what you do when that storm comes."
Alexander Dumas, from *The Count of Monti Cristo*

Table of Contents

Acknowledgments. ix
Introduction. 1
Chapter 1: Allegations and Responses. 13
Chapter 2: Fawcett and Greenwood. 18
Chapter 3: Charles, Larry, and Peter. 34
Chapter 4: The Colonel vs. *Left At East Gate*. 45
Chapter 5: A Walk In the Forest. 55
Chapter 6: Anomalous Injuries. 63
Chapter 7: The Underground. 73
Chapter 8: The Colonel vs. *Left At East Gate,* Part II. 88
Chapter 9: "They Talk About Cloud Busters". 93
Chapter 10: Halt and Hopkins. 103
Chapter 11: On Being 'Meddled' With and a Certain Suicide. 119
Chapter 12: Regarding Adrian Bustinza. 134
Chapter 13: "Let's Talk About Soil Analysis". 144
Chapter 14: Closing Remarks. 158
Conclusions. 162
About the Author. 178

Acknowledgments

For their active assistance throughout the writing of this book and for their continuing contributions to our collective understanding of what happened in the Rendlesham Forest in December 1980, I thank you all, in alphabetical order.

Colin Andrews, Betty Andreasson, John Burroughs, Adrian C. Bustinza III, Jimmy Church, Pat Colligan, Richard Dolan, Ronnie Dugdale, Alyson Dunlop, Paul Eno, Gordon (Gordy) Goodger, Barry Greenwood, Gary Heseltine, Race Hobbs, David M. Jacobs, Ben Emlyn-Jones, Tiberius Kirk, Robert Luca, Jim Macmillan, Jon Marsden, Marty Martin, Sue McAllister, Steve Mera, Matthew Moniz, Linda Moulton-Howe, Allan Robbins, Lou Ann Robinson, Robert Salas, Jennifer Stein, Larry Warren and Martin Willis. With apologies to those I may have forgotten.

Introduction

"I'm tired of him putting lies out. You need to know the truth. The problem with ufology is there's too much nonsense out there. It needs scientific investigation by competent people, and not a whole lot of nonsense. That's my big frustration and that's probably one of the main reasons I'm here tonight."
—Col. (ret) Charles I Halt, Woodbridge Suffolk, 11 July 2015

"When the game is lost, slander becomes the tool of the loser."
—Socrates

A street in Woodbridge, Suffolk

The town of Woodbridge is located in Suffolk East Anglia. That's in the southeast corner of England, about a two-hour drive from London. Woodbridge is the closest town (though there are closer villages) to a series of locations where the world's best-known and most significant military/UFO encounter too place occurred. The Rendlesham Forest UFO incident (RFI) took place on three consecutive nights between Christmas and New Years 1980. Numerous United States Air Force personnel witnessed or were otherwise involved in these events with some involved more than once. The Ministry of

Defence, the Air Force, and another agency or two managed to keep the lid battened down until the story broke internationally in October 1983.

Since then the Rendlesham Forest incident has remained the

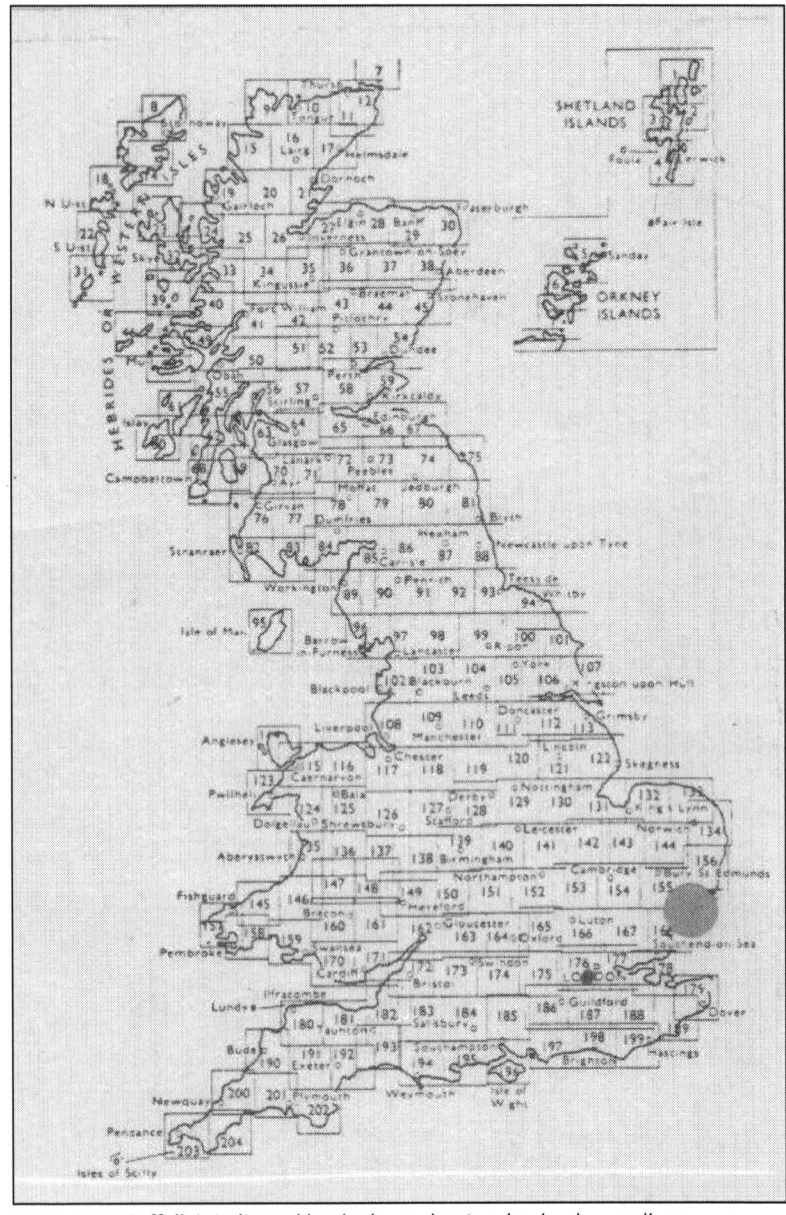

Suffolk is indicated by the large dot, London by the smaller.

Introduction

most hotly debated and intently followed UFO incident since Roswell. Books have been written about it and hundreds of articles as well. How many Rendlesham posts, questions, challenges and arguments have made their way into internet chat rooms ad onto UFO websites, Facebook pages and other internet destinations is anyone's guess. The assortment of theories it has given rise to range from the truly perceptive and thoughtful to the mind-numbingly idiotic. New 'breaks' in the case are discussed and argued over while an ever-growing international audience does its best to educate itself about the Rendlesham Forest incident.

Lt. Col. Charles I. Halt, photo, early 1980s

Over the years some of the original witnesses, joined by a small cadre of investigators, researchers and authors, have done their best to keep the focus where it should be: on the testimony of the witnesses themselves, the documented physical evidence, military paper trail, letters, photographs, emails, and other court-worthy evidence supporting the physical reality of the events. Then there are those who will always act to cloud the waters, this while insisting they are only trying to clarify them. The carefully skewed data they inject into the mix is called disinformation, and the most recent example came in the form of a talk given on Saturday11 July at the Woodbridge Community Building. The speaker was Charles I. Halt, a retired United States Air Force colonel who had been the Deputy Base Commander of RAF Bentwaters at the time of the December 1980 UFO events.

Wikipedia, a sometimes dubious resource I almost never consult but believe to be accurate here, states: "Charles I. Halt (Born 1939) is a retired United States Air Force colonel and the former base commander of RAF Bentwaters, near Woodbridge, Suffolk. After serving in Vietnam, Japan and Korea, he was assigned to Bentwaters as deputy commander. The Rendlesham Forest incident of late December 1980 occurred shortly afterwards, and he was an important witness to events on the second night (actually third night) of sightings. After retiring from the US Air Force in 1991, Halt made his first public appearance in a television documentary, where he confirmed the authenticity of the Rendlesham Forest incident."

Larry Warren was born in New York City in 1961 and grew up in New York State's lower Hudson River region. He enlisted in the Air Force in November 1979 and commenced basic training following his graduation from high school in the summer of 1980. Warren was inspired to join the military in great part by the then ongoing Iranian Hostage Crisis. He trained to be a USAF Security Police Specialist (SPS) and served in that capacity at RAF Bentwaters. He left the service with a (fully) honorable discharge in May 1981. Larry Warren was the event's whistle-blower, the first of the witnesses to break security –and by many years at that. He was the first to make public many of the specifics of the incident he'd been involved in, contact information for other witnesses, and what he'd learned of the other events. In 1983 a Freedom of Information Act action (FOIA) based on information from Warren resulted in the

Introduction

Security Police Specialist, Airman First Class Lawrence P. Warren, RAF Bentwaters, spring 1981.

release of a single-page USAF memorandum. It was written by then-Lt. Col. Halt and confirmed that different UFO events had occurred. For almost twenty years this memo was the only document to officially verify the reality of the Rendlesham Forest UFO incident:

The FOIA itself was filed by Larry Fawcett, a Coventry Connecticut police lieutenant and UFO investigator, and Barry Greenwood, a UFO researcher and archivist. They were aided by Robert Todd chief researcher at the time for CAUS – 'Citizen's Against UFO Secrecy.' In early 1983 Fawcett became the first person to interview Warren.

I don't think for a second that Col. Halt would have written and signed such a document by choice. But he wasn't given a choice. The 'Unexplained Lights' memo was written and filed as a 'courtesy' to the Ministry of Defence with no record of it

> **DEPARTMENT OF THE AIR FORCE**
> HEADQUARTERS 81ST COMBAT SUPPORT GROUP (USAFE)
> APO NEW YORK 09755
>
> REPLY TO ATTN OF: CD
>
> 13 Jan 81
>
> SUBJECT: Unexplained Lights
>
> TO: RAF/CC
>
> 1. Early in the morning of 27 Dec 80 (approximately 0300L), two USAF security police patrolmen saw unusual lights outside the back gate at RAF Woodbridge. Thinking an aircraft might have crashed or been forced down, they called for permission to go outside the gate to investigate. The on-duty flight chief responded and allowed three patrolmen to proceed on foot. The individuals reported seeing a strange glowing object in the forest. The object was described as being metallic in appearance and triangular in shape, approximately two to three meters across the base and approximately two meters high. It illuminated the entire forest with a white light. The object itself had a pulsing red light on top and a bank(s) of blue lights underneath. The object was hovering or on legs. As the patrolmen approached the object, it maneuvered through the trees and disappeared. At this time the animals on a nearby farm went into a frenzy. The object was briefly sighted approximately an hour later near the back gate.
>
> 2. The next day, three depressions 1 1/2" deep and 7" in diameter were found where the object had been sighted on the ground. The following night (29 Dec 80) the area was checked for radiation. Beta/gamma readings of 0.1 milliroentgens were recorded with peak readings in the three depressions and near the center of the triangle formed by the depressions. A nearby tree had moderate (.05-.07) readings on the side of the tree toward the depressions.
>
> 3. Later in the night a red sun-like light was seen through the trees. It moved about and pulsed. At one point it appeared to throw off glowing particles and then broke into five separate white objects and then disappeared. Immediately thereafter, three star-like objects were noticed in the sky, two objects to the north and one to the south, all of which were about 10° off the horizon. The objects moved rapidly in sharp angular movements and displayed red, green and blue lights. The objects to the north appeared to be elliptical through an 8-12 power lens. They then turned to full circles. The objects to the north remained in the sky for an hour or more. The object to the south was visible for two or three hours and beamed down a stream of light from time to time. Numerous individuals, including the undersigned, witnessed the activities in paragraphs 2 and 3.
>
> CHARLES I. HALT, Lt Col, USAF
> Deputy Base Commander

Lt. Col. Halt's 'Unexplained Lights' memo of 13 January 1981.

turning up in Air Force files during the FOIA investigation. Upon the release of the memo Fawcett sent a copy of to a colleague in England. That colleague shared it with another colleague. He in turn sold it to the News of the World, The largest tabloid newspaper in the world. The copy of the Halt memo fetched twenty five thousand dollars or twenty five thousand pounds, memories differ. But not a cent of it made its way back to Charles Halt, Larry Warren, or Fawcett and Greenwood.

The News of the World broke the story on Sunday 2 October 1983, its front page prominently featuring both Charles Halt's memo and Charles Halt's name. From that day on his name would always be linked to the UFO landing in Suffolk. Larry Warren was also featured from the first day on, but as 'the airman Art Wallace,' a pseudonym created by one of the original investigators.

Public knowledge of the incident brought unwanted attention, ridicule, and very real intrusions into Col. Halt's personal life. It did not help his military career either. This officer had already been approved for advancement at the time of the RFI and was promoted to full colonel almost immediately afterward, though never to advance another rank. To this day Charles has publicly maintained that he holds no personal grudge or ill will toward Larry as the person directly responsible for derailing a good part of his life. With respect, this is something I find difficult to believe.

My reasons for writing this book are best summed up in the colonel's words, "I'm tired of him putting lies out. You need to know the truth." Our only difference of opinion being who the "him" referred to is.

For me the extra-large straw that broke the camel's back came during the final thirty or so minutes of Mr. Halt's 'presentation.' It was exclusively devoted to a non-stop attack on the character, word, integrity, motivations, honesty and good name of my friend and co-author Larry Warren. The speaker also focused his ire on my basic competence as an investigative writer and the accuracy and integrity of the book we wrote together, *Left At East Gate: A First-Hand Account of the Rendlesham Forest UFO Incident, Its Cover-Up and Investigation*.

The first edition of "Left At East Gate," Published in 1997 by Marlowe & Company, New York City, and Michael O'Mara Books Ltd., London.

In responding to the colonel's list of our alleged errors, mistakes, general dishonesty, conflicting accounts and assorted lies, I felt I had no recourse but to answer each of them point by point, and in as much evidence-driven detail as I felt necessary to fully refute the charge. That turned out to be a considerably larger task than I'd first imagined. While this most recent attack

Introduction

was indeed in a class by itself, it was also just the latest, if most over-the-top attempt to destroy Warren's credibility in what has been a calculated, ongoing, three-decades-long series of assaults on one of the most important military/UFO whistle-blowers in history. As I began to study each of the accusations on its own, I saw in microcosm the entire sweep of an ongoing thirty-year plus campaign to discredit a decent and courageous man. That's what this book is about.

The expanded edition of "Left At East Gate" published in 2005 by Cosimo Books, New York City. Cover illustrations, Sal Amendola.

The opportunity for Mr. Halt to mount this attack came in the form of an invitation to return to England to speak about the Rendlesham Forest incident. The invitation was extended by the conference's organizer, English UFO author and researcher John Hanson. this in association with conference co-organizer and MC, David Bryant. The talk had originally been promoted as the "Col. Halt Woodbridge Briefing" with the name changed to

Halt in Woodbridge

"Haunted Skies Conference. Colonel Halt is coming to Woodbridge Community Hall Suffolk."

I'm guessing the name change reflected the sponsorship of Hanson, publisher of the *Haunted Skies* book series, now up to number 11. Volume Eight, published in 2013, is entirely dedicated to UK UFO events of 1980 with a particular focus on the RFI, bolstered by additional information on other anomalous events also occurring that year. In Hanson's words:

> "In respect of (Volume 8 -1980) we consulted on many occasions with Colonel Charles Halt, who was the Deputy Base Commander. He not only agreed to assist us but has recommended the value of reading our books, which we regard as a privilege. In addition to this, we have outlined various examples of what may well be regarded as paranormal phenomena, which is still taking place in the forest to this present day."

Some months prior to the talk, word went out that the speaker would not be taking or answering any questions about the remarks he would be making that day. Not long afterward Larry Warren, first night witness John Burroughs, selected other RFI witnesses and myself learned we would not be welcome to attend, even if we paid our twenty pound entry fee. This led to my contacting John Hanson and asking him to relay a brief message to Mr. Halt for me. It was, if I were able to attend (I wasn't), would I be allowed entry if I gave him my word not to make a scene or disrupt the proceedings, neither of which I'm known for. Charles responded in the affirmative and retracted the 'ban' on me and me alone. There's no question though that had I attended, and had he given the talk he did, I would most certainly would have been ejected from that hall.

I was able to view the entire talk via a link provided by Ben Emlyn-Jones, an Oxford-based radio host who had been asked to record the lecture by Mr. Hanson. Ben filmed the entire talk from his tripod-mounted video camera in full view of all from the front stage-right side line. The video was posted on YouTube, but Emlyn-Jones was forced to remove it a few days later due to a dubious charge of copyright infringement. The charge was made by David but dismissed as without merit by YouTube officials. Ben's video and part of the 'walk in the Rendlesham Forest' returned to YouTube as parts of a documentary on the event. On 13 August surprisingly even-handed article on this brief 'go-to' was posted on line by the writer who goes by the name of 'Gilly.'[1]

I suggest in the strongest possible terms that readers take the time to view and listen to the colonel's talk either beforehand or as they progress in their reading. Given my partisan position in all this it's important that you be able to verify for yourselves that I haven't misrepresented or in any way biased my responses against Mr. Halt.

The reason some of the colonel's transcribed remarks seem fragmented is because Emlyn-Jones' camera was unable to pick up all of the dialogue and the audio system in the hall was found wanting. If I've misinterpreted a word or phrase as a result it was unintentional. If I were stupid enough to have done so and caught by a wary reader my reputation as an investigative writer would suffer deservedly.

During this investigation I've repeatedly returned to the text of both editions of *Left At East Gate* as well as relevant documents, memos, letters, maps, reports, Air Force manuals, photographs, testimony, transcripts, recorded conversations and part of Larry's service record. Every one of Mr. Halt's charges are reviewed and responded to here with not a single one missed or edited out. I had one major my goal in writing this. These attacks need to be seen for what they are, and they need to stop, and stop for good. It's my hope that the documented information in this book will help to do just that.

Had the colonel decided to leave public life with a talk dedicated to what he and his men experienced, then gone on to

---

[1] You can find it at http://www.anythingexcepthousework.co.uk/copyright-claim-victory-on-youtube/. The full video can be accessed at https://www.youtube.com/watch?v=Dh3uJl0Olgl. The final part of his talk begins about two hours and twenty-seven minutes into the YouTube upload.

share his thoughts, comments, reflections and memories from his unique vantage as a command officer, he could have left the stage with his head held relatively high. What a shame he decided to add character assassination and disinformation to his list of subjects. It's not without some irony that the only person worthy of our admiration and respect at the end of this story is the attacked, not attacker, and in no uncertain terms.

Peter Robbins
New York City
4 September 2015

Chapter 1:
Allegations and Responses

Note: All of the presenter's allegations and relevant comments are highlighted in **bold.**

Two years go by…1983…a young man we put out of the service – we can talk about that a little later. He was unsuitable, undesirable. He asked for a discharge. You can verify that. We did give him honorable discharge, but he was literally booted out. Picked up the story from Adrian Bustinza apparently… documentation on that…from some of the other cops.

Let's take the colonel's statements one at a time, beginning with "a young man we put out the service…"

"Unsuitable?" "Undesirable?" Certainly to anyone interested in keeping UFO event-related information from the public, especially as coming from a USAF Security Specialist who refused to follow orders or do what he was told. In Larry's words, "I knew I was breaking the rules, but I just didn't care." (*LAEG,* page 55). And yes, unsuitable and undesirable to someone looking to get back at the person who had done more to bring unwanted attention to their military career and personal life.

Fully acknowledging Mr. Halt's many achievements during his twenty-plus years in the Air Force, the currently serving and former USAF personnel I've spoken with over the years concur that, all things being equal, he should have left as a brigadier (one star general) at the least. Base Wing Commander Colonel Gordon Williams, also caught up in the events of 12/80, but who managed to keep his head down in its aftermath, retired as a two-star. Williams in fact "…had scored his first star and was going to Germany after only a year and a half at Bentwaters (*LAEG*, page 72). No one but the brass involved in deciding on his advancement or lack of same can tell us with any certainty why he remained a colonel. Alternately, no one can deny that the wrench Larry Warren threw into his career in 1983 may well have been the deciding factor. The Air Force does not look kindly upon officers *or* enlisted personnel who get their names publically associated with the subject of UFOs, however it happens to come about.

Suffolk newspapers the Evening Star and the East Anglian Daily Times cover a return visit to the area by Col. Halt, aka "UFO man." Both these articles were published on Halloween 1984.

But otherwise "unsuitable" or "undesirable?" Not in the least. There is nothing outside of Warren's ongoing quest to learn

Chapter 1: Allegations and Responses

more, about the events he and others had been involved in, and about what had been done to them. Specific examples? Six days after Lt. Col. Halt wrote and filed his 'Unexplained Lights' memo, Warren received orders naming him to join a highly select group of Security Police and K-9 units for an historical assignment. They were flown to Ramstein Air Force Base in West Germany to provide security and crowd control for the just-released American hostages about to arrive there from Iran. They had been held prisoner there for four hundred and forty four days (*LAEG,* page 66). This assignment was made and accepted with the understanding that complete secrecy had to be observed. The public announcement was timed to follow the next day, immediately after the inauguration of President Elect Ronald Reagan. Not the kind of assignment you would pick a 'loose cannon' for.

Two months after this Warren was selected to be an honor guard for Wing Commander Gordon Williams testimonial, secure general officers' parking for William's change of command ceremony on the base flight line. Additionally, Warren acted as Williams' driver at one point and also served as part of his security detail. (*LAEG, page 72*).

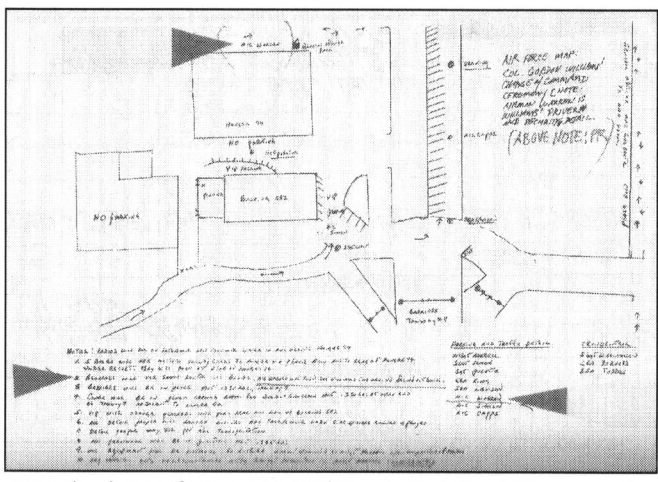

Note the three references to AIC (Airman First Class) Warren on the map/orders issued to personnel involved in Wing Commander Williams' change of command ceremony.

During the time he served with the 81st Security Police at Bentwaters the squadron received a unit citation as the best SPS in USAFE (United States Air Forces in Europe). Granted, this was not a personal citation but Charles Halt's "unsuitable" and "undesirable" remarks are completely without merit or support.

He asked for a discharge. You can verify that. We did give him honorable discharge, but he was literally booted out.

Here the colonel freely acknowledges that Warren had requested a discharge and that it was granted. He then tells the audience that "he was literally booted out." What is the source of this extremely serious allegation?

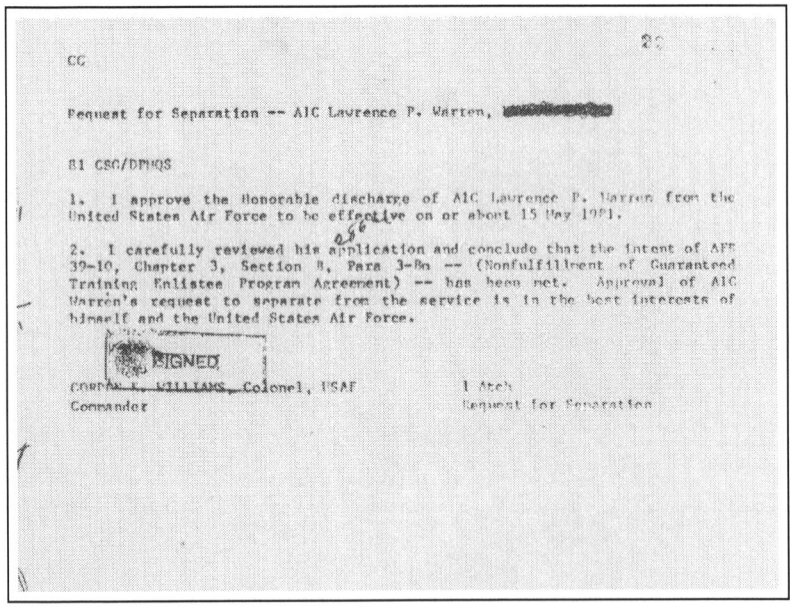

Warren's April 22 1981 Request for Separation.

Regarding the colonel's claim, note the specific wording on Warren's 22 April 'Request for Separation' as written by the officer who approved it, none other than Base Wing Commander

Williams. Such a routine procedure would normally never have fallen to the base wing commander, but instead handled by base office personnel. What does Col. Williams have to say here? "I carefully reviewed his application and conclude that the intent of AFR (Air Force regulation) 39-10, Chapter 3, Section B, Para 3-8a, Nonfulfillmet of Guaranteed Training Enlistee Program Agreement, has been met. Approval of AIC Warren's request to separate from the service is in the best interests of himself and the United States Air Force." Translation: The Air Force had broken their guaranteed contract with Larry Warren, not the other way around. In no way can this be interpreted as his having been "literally booted out" of the Air Force. The honorable discharge he received in May 1981 was honorable in all respects.

Picked up the story from Adrian Bustinza apparently (inaudible) documentation on that...from some of the other cops...suddenly put himself into the story."

Halt has other things to say about Security Specialist, Sgt. Adrian Bustinza, also assigned to D Flight. I've chosen to consolidate almost all of Col. Halt's references to Sgt. Bustinza until further along in the book.

Chapter 2:
Fawcett and Greenwood

He went back to the States...ran in to a couple of people who were writing a story, *Clear Intent*. Maybe some of you have read. Larry Fawcett and Barry Greenwood, two great guys. Well, they pick him up and they're all, 'well, here's a case we can't pass up. We're gonna put this in our book. It's gonna be the crown jewel of the book. They did work with him, and he finally confesses to them he was lying. I have that in writing from Barry, and orally from Larry.

Greenwood, eh, Larry Fawcett. He contacts me – Larry Fawcett does – and I said "Well, I'll help you with the book if you keep it honest and straight forward and stick with the facts. We signed an agreement. I sent them off. Well, they lost interest in that book. Larry Warren told them and all the problems. There were issues about my memo, my tape. It got sold to the Japanese. It got (to the newspaper) News of the World. It got so (unclear: deluded?) no one knew what was going on. They said 'I'm not convinced,' and they backed off. They put a bid in (for?) *Clear Intent*,' didn't cover it fully. So, yeah, I thought it was pretty much closed.

Warren returned to Glens Falls New York in May 1981. The Post Traumatic Stress he left the service with only continued to intensify and the toll it took on him was not a pretty one. In January 1981 he hit a dangerously low point. In his painfully honest words, "I spent my days and nights with people lost in drugs and alcohol. My mother and I hadn't spoken for weeks. I found myself getting into some bizarre situations with women, but unable to communicate with any of them. While I was frustrated with people accepting the norm and blinding themselves to what really was going on, I was doing a fine job of that on myself." (*LAEG* page 87)

Thankfully he did talk with his mother soon after this. Joann Warren, a strong, smart, caring woman who will always have my admiration, affection and respect, suggested that he talk to his father, the couple divorced for some years by then. After agreeing to his dad's house rules, Larry, now twenty-one years old, moved in with him and his father's second wife Sandy to restart his life in Hartford Connecticut. (*LAEG,* page 89). He never "ran into" Larry Fawcett and Barry Greenwood. He was introduced to them by well-known UFO abductee Betty Andraesson and her husband Bob Luca. Larry had learned of the couple through an interview they did for the *Hartford Courant* newspaper. The reporter noted (with Bob's permission) that he worked at Middletown Toyota which was where Larry first contacted him, right after having had dental surgery. (*LAEG,* page 92).

Bob Luca remembers this time particularly well:

> "I received a phone call at my job from Larry who explained to me that he had been in the military and was witness to a UFO incident while on active service. To be honest I did not know if I believed him or not. As it turned out Larry had just had dental work done and his speech was kind of strange and since we had been pranked before by jokers I really did not know what to make of this person on the other end of the phone line. I decided that if there was a chance he was legitimate it certainly would be worth talking to him and invited him to come to our home. As it turned out this was a wise choice.
>
> Larry arrived at our home at the time agreed upon. He turned out to be very friendly, serious, likable, and obviously sincere person. There was no doubt in my mind after that. He was relating to us an event in his life exactly as he remembered it. We spent hours listening to and recording Larry's explanation of what he saw as and viewing the diagrams he drew for us. Now there was a problem for Betty and I as I realized we did not have the experience to truly look into this unique case. That was when we decided to put Larry in touch with Larry Fawcett, a police lieutenant and UFO investigator involved in our case. Larry (Fawcett) and Barry Greenwood, a Massachusetts UFO investigator, were both heavily involved in investigating and penning a book on the government's UFO cover

up. Since Fawcett was one of the founders of CAUS (Citizens Against UFO Secrecy) they had access to attorneys and researchers who could do Larry more good than we could.

As time went on I wrote the British Ministry of Defence and questioned them about the Bentwaters UFO incident. The reply was as expected, stating in their letter that the whole story was a hoax. I also filed FOIA on the US Air Force. They responded that as a non-event no investigation was undertaken. Today of course we know it was the Ministry of Defence and the Air Force that were lying and not Larry Warren.

Larry's contacting us and the resulting story that came out due to the research and hard work of CAUS, coupled with the bravery of Larry Warren and co-author Peter Robbins in bringing this forth was just one more reason the powers that be were and remain upset with us. The story of the Rendlesham Forest UFO incident from the perspective of the event's whistle-blower is told in the excellent and highly-detailed book by Larry Warren and Peter Robbins titled *Left at East Gate*."[2]

This is something you need to know about Larry Warren in the two to three years after Rendlesham. Larry Warren made the decision to go public with what he knew only days after the events themselves. The when and how would sort themselves out later on. The agreement he made with himself as a nineteen years old was this. When speaking with anyone other than men who had been involved, only talk about the most outrageous-sounding episodes, the underground, the beings, as having come from to 'a guy or guys I knew,' not himself, despite the fact they had. He did this for two reasons. To protect himself and his family from the incredulous reactions others would surely have about such an explosive series of admissions. Second, in the hope it would draw out Adrian Bustinza, the person who he had shared the majority of these experiences with, to go public. We

---

[2](Note: The above is part of a working chapter draft of a book-in-progress by Betty Andraesson and Bob Luca. The couple's experiences have been the subject of three books by the respected author Raymond Fowler, *The Andreasson Affair, The Andreasson Affair: Phase Two,* and *The Andreasson Legacy*)

now know how little chance there was of Adrian doing so back then, though more about this later. Larry took this 'guys I know' stance in the letter he wrote home to his family within a week after the events. It told them much of what had actually happened but not in the first-person, He took the same course with Larry Fawcett and Barry Greenwood in 1984, and in 1987, with me. In Fawcett and Greenwood's case his attempted backtracking resulted in the detailing of their work relationship. Why? Because 'Larry Warren had 'changed his story.'

Please remember we are talking about a truly courageous, PTSD'ed-out idealistic twenty-two year old who had gone through an unimaginably frightening, disorienting, life-changing experience. And how did he respond? By putting everything he had on the line and going up against the secrecy-keeping apparatus of the United States Air Force, the American intelligence community, and almost inevitable isolation in the court of public opinion, and for the rest of his life as it's turned out. Why would anyone choose to follow the path that Warren did? Because there are people in this world called whistle-blowers. Authentic ones are few and far between and they differ from the rest of us. My best sense is that in my co–author's case his parents instilled an extraordinarily acute sense of right and wrong in him as a kid. He also suffers from the conviction that when you see a wrong being done it should be addressed.

I think what happened with Fawcett and Greenwood was that Warren found himself caught between his desire to tell them the truth and get the information out there, and the equally strong impulse to protect himself, his family, and the parts of his account it was most important that people take seriously. But he was now working with a police officer experienced in observing and questioning. He was also under the scrutiny of an extremely knowledgeable scholar-level archivist-ufologist, neither of whom had ever heard of an account like his before. More, some of the actual, truly experienced things Warren was telling them were still infused with some of the false memories put in his head during whatever Disneyland-on-acid 'debriefing' he and others were made to endure. The real disconnect with Fawcett and Greenwood came when the former caught him off his guard and started to really push, to the effect of, you saw more, didn't you. At that point Warren admitted same while immediately regretting it. The result, he felt compelled to back out of his admission saying it had happened to 'a guy or guys I knew.' This turnabout was enough for Fawcett and Greenwood, though the pair took Warren's core account as truthful enough to include in their completed manuscript for *Clear Intent*.

Charles Halt contacted Barry Greenwood last July, primarily wanting to know if he would be interested in writing a book about Rendlesham from the colonel's point of view which Barry was not interested in. Also to pick the ufologist's mind about discrepancies in Larry Warren's account. The colonel would do the same a few months later with the noted UFO abduction researcher, Dr. David Jacobs. Greenwood responded to Halt's questions in this 15 July 2014 email:

"Chuck,

Yes, I recall those days. Larry [Fawcett] passed away a couple of years ago. In fact, a number of old friends have passed, including my mother, in recent times but I try to keep busy.

Larry Warren had surfaced in Connecticut, probably around 1982 and contacted Larry F. with the version of the story we mentioned. There was little on Bentwaters circulating at the time but I recalled seeing a small piece in the British "Flying Saucer Review" that sounded like the story Larry W alluded to. Because of that, Larry W seemed to have inside information on it and he was interviewed. He was rather nervous, or seemed so, about being identified so I gave him a pseudonym, Art Wallace, which made him more comfortable. I would have long conversations on the phone after work at night with many questions. I was having a problem with the way his story was evolving as it became bizarre and my pressing with questions must have revealed my increasing issues with those details. One evening on the phone Larry W decided to confess his non-involvement in part of the story (seeing aliens, underground facility, etc.). He said he was relating what actually happened to Adrian

Bustinza in an effort to more or less flush out Bustinza to tell his part of the story as it actually happened to him. It didn't happen as Larry hoped, which is why he fessed up. I told Larry this was a real problem and he was going to have to answer for it.

In the meantime Bentwaters began to evolve on its own with others surfacing in the UK. Our colleague, Robert Todd, had filed FOIA requests on the story because of what Larry F and I had passed along from Larry W and a few scraps of other short accounts. Your memo turned up, oddly via the MOD as the staffer who handled the request couldn't find it in AF records and sent a request to the MOD for a copy. This went above and beyond what FOIA defined but am glad he did. Besides Larry W's confession, the following is where the story really went south for Larry F and I.

I sent a copy of your memo to Jenny Randles, who as you recall was one of the British side of looking into the report. The purpose was to help them unearth further information on their end with concrete information instead of rumour. We were previously blasted out by Brenda Butler, another British investigator, for getting involved in what she thought was their story. But I knew Jenny and trusted her to use the document to cleanly reveal more as it did no good to sit on it here. A while later the News of the World newspaper came out with a huge expose and, unknown to us here, Jenny showed the memo to a BUFORA member, Harry Harris, who was a solicitor. He decided to cash in on the story by selling the details, and the memo contents to the paper for a large sum of money. I understand that Jenny, Brenda and Dot Street received something like $2000 or 2000 pounds each with Harris pocketing the rest. I attended the 1987 MUFON conference in Washington D.C. where Jenny was speaking. I didn't know all these details at the time and was milling around in a hall with a crowd. I ran into Jenny who couldn't seem to look me in the eye and was extremely apologetic. A small group of people had gathered around us as if they knew something I didn't. We discussed what happened and after this all my interest in the story evaporated. Our main witness misled us and the British side went bad with what I can only call corruption by BUFORA's solicitor and what used to be called "payola" in selling the information we unearthed to a British tabloid. It was an entirely unethical use of the information we

Halt in Woodbridge

developed on our end.

I told Larry F that I've had it with this investigation as we couldn't afford to have a taint of what I described above sticking to us. I was trying to make the subject of UFO document research respectable by being careful with what was done with unearthed documentation since there had already been many hoaxes circulating prior to this. Obviously, this wasn't to be the case the way this was going.

Barry Greenwood"

I spoke with Barry about all this in August. We hadn't been in contact for five years. Before that, maybe twenty years. I can understand why he Larry Fawcett decided to move on when they did. The whole idea of such a scenario just seemed so 'far out' in 1983. And it was. Thirty plus years ago. The whole Rendlesham ball of wax can be summed up in a favorite line from Oliver Stone's "JFK." Assassination conspirator David Ferry, brilliantly portrayed by Joe Pesci, observes of the conspiracy: "It's a riddle wrapped in a mystery wrapped in an enigma." I think that's the order.

What follows is the letter Airman Warren wrote home on 6 January 1981, the first four pages are not included as they only address personal matters. A page of transcription is missing here but the actual handwritten page is included, as well as the rest of what Airman Warren wrote home that day:

Larry Warren's letter to home, envelope.

Chapter 2: Fawcett and Greenwood

"Dear Ma, Sam & Mike,

How's things at home -- I hope good -- I am o.k.

Please don't be too upset that it has taken me so long to write. I think that was because I told you all I was doing on the phone and could not think of anything to say.

... Remember I was telling you about that U.F.O. that landed (*this during a prohibited phone call he had made to his mother the day after the third night's event*) -- well I'll tell you the whole story on it. Over Europe and England a bunch of lights were seen -- Over London one of the lights broke into about twenty smaller lights -and flew in all directions. At about three in the morning, a guy I know in D-Flight of Security Police told me he responded to a falling star outside the Weapons Storage Area -- I can't tell you what they keep in there but use your imagination! Anyway he reported it and then everyone started feeling strange -- then a guy on the Backgate at Woodbridge reported a bright light moving through the pine forest. An officer and two sergeants responded but they could not take weapons because they were off base.

Over the radio they reported seeing a pie-shaped object -- about 7 by 8 ft in size. But they said every time they would get near it, it would seem farther away all of a sudden. They also said that all of the animals in the forest were going nuts.

Then all of a sudden the light went out -- and over the radio they said they didn't like the situation and wanted to go back to base -- but they were told to keep on investigating.

Then they said the thing appeared behind them -- it seemed like it was playing games. After 3 and a half miles of following the thing through the countryside and woods -- the thing just disappeared in a field -it was only about 10 ft off the ground. This is what a friend of mine said he heard on the radio.

At that same time, me and five other guys were walking up a dark path about 2 miles from base cause we couldn't get a ride and we felt like we were being watched and it was strange cause there were no street lights -- Then we saw a bright light go right over us about 50 ft up and just fly over a field.

It was silent. We first thought it was an A-10 Jet. But they scream. So we ran away, because witchcraft and black magic is big in this part of Suffolk and we thought that witches were in the woods. That light just seemed to jump over the trees -- Then the next day it turned out that we were in the same place as the U.F.O. so I think we saw it too. Now the three people who saw it can't and won't talk about it at all. And supposedly no animals have gone back into the woods yet -- They did find two landing sights -- and supposedly some equipment left behind.

A big C-130 came in and took something in a crate away a few days later and the guards were flown in from somewhere else -- it is strange, and now I hear that strange things have been going on in the forest for the past weeks -- and remember we <u>did</u> get cut off on the phone... Say hi to everyone and I'll call soon."

Love, Larry

P.S. The picture is of me in London about a month ago ... tell Sam to write.

(P.S. Ma, When I get home I'll tell you the truth about the U.F.O.: I can't in the mail, they read it!)

Chapter 2: Fawcett and Greenwood

> Remember I was telling you about that
> U.F.O. that Sanchel? Well I'll
> Tell you the Whole Story on it.
> Over Europe and England a bunch
> of lights were seen - over London
> one of the lights Broke into about
> 20 smaller lights - and flew in all
> directions. at about 3 in the morning.
> a guy I knew in A flight of security police told me
> he spotted a falling star at side
> of the Weapon Storage area - I can't tell
> you what they keep in there But use your
> Imigination! anyway he reported it
> and then Everyone started feeling
> strange - Then a guy on the Backgate
> at Woodbridge reported a Bright
> light moving through the pine forest
> an officer and two sargets responded
> But they could not take Weapons Because
> they were off Base.
> Over the Radio they reported seeing
> a pie shaped object - about 7 by 8 ft in size
> But they said Every Time they would
> get near it, it would seem farther
> away all of a sudden.

Larry Warren's letter home. First page of UFO story.

27

They also said that all of the animals in the forest were going nuts. Then all of a sudden the lights went out - and opened the radio the said They didn't like the situation and wanted to go Back to Base - But They were told to keep on investigating. Then they said the thing appeared Behind them - it seemed like it was playing games. After 3 and ½ miles of following the thing, through country side and woods - the thing just disappeared in a field - It was only about 10 ft of the ground. This is what a friend of mine had he heard on the radio - At that same time me and 5 other guys were walking up a dark road about 2 miles from Base coming Back from Ipswith - cause we couldn't get a ride. And we felt like we were Being watched and it was strange cause there were no street lights - Then we saw a Bright light go right over us about 50 ft up - and just fly over a field

Larry Warren's letter home. Second page of UFO story.

Chapter 2: Fawcett and Greenwood

> It was silent. We first thought it
> was an A-10 Jet. But they scream.
> So we ran away. Because witchcraft
> and Black Magic is Big in this part of
> Suffolk — and we thought that witches
> were in the woods — Because that light
> just seemed to jump over the
> trees — The next day it turned
> out we were in the same place as
> the U.F.O. So I think we saw it to.
> Now the three people who shared it
> can't and won't talk about it at all.
> And supposedly no animals have gone
> Back into the Wood yet. They did find
> Two landing sights and supposedly
> some equiptment left behind.
> A Big C-130 came in and took some Thing
> in a crate away a few days later
> and the guards were flown
> in from somewere else — it is strange
> and new to hear that strange things
> have been going on in the forest
> for the past few weeks —
> and remember we did get out of
> on the shore.

Larry Warren's letter home. Third page of UFO story.

Halt in Woodbridge

Larry Warren's letter home. Final page.

Larry had learned an important lesson in the arc of his relationship with Fawcett and Greenwood and did not intend to repeat what had happened with them with me. Our 'business agreement' consisted of a handshake in the summer of 1987 (until an actual contract was drawn up in 1996), but it was not until April 1988 that he felt it was relatively safe to share the missing pieces with me, and in my case he had judged correctly. In fact what he told me that night changed my life forever:

> "The call from Larry came about eight one night. I picked up the receiver on the second ring and turned off the television immediately; it was something about his voice. There were a few things about Bentwaters he'd been wanting to tell me, and it was time I knew about them. Not that he hadn't trusted me but "I just didn't know if you could handle it." He hoped I could now. Buckle your seatbelt, I thought.
>
> I had never recorded any of our telephone calls, but the impulse to grab a recorder, cassette, and phone jack was immediate. I didn't, though. I just kept my seat and listened. What Larry had to say might fill in that "big blank," and I didn't want to miss a word.
>
> One at a time, Larry calmly described a series of incidents I was

not familiar with. The first began with a phone call, a car ride, and an elevator descent. As he talked, I watched the hair on my arms rise. The underground was real and Larry had been there. He was not sure for how long. Adrian's standing account was actually a combination of both their memories: "A guy I knew" could mean "me," and I was walked through it all now.

Other particulars followed. These included the beings he'd seen approach us in the field by the base that night. Then about his contacts with NSA personnel. News that I'd been the subject of some Agency background check, then "okayed" to work with Larry, left me feeling momentarily nauseous. He was sure our phones were irregularly monitored and had been from the start. Other calls we'd made might have been similarly intercepted. What was left of my Bentwaters innocence drained away with each new revelation. Was this really happening? I couldn't believe he was talking about this on the phone. Mightn't this be one of those monitored calls, I awkwardly suggested. If anyone were listening in, he offered, it was them, and they already knew all about it.

A warning bell was going off inside me. Forget about Larry -- given only what I'd experienced, learned, or thought I'd learned about Bentwaters on my own, <u>nothing</u> he was saying sounded out of the question, and that was not a good feeling. If he was one of those rare people with the compulsion -- and ability -- to lie so spectacularly, I still wasn't getting it. And by this time, I was starting to wish I would get it: Larry as liar was preferable to these things being true. Forget about the book. I had just been debriefed on how far in over my head I had gotten myself. What frightened me most was I believed him. I never went to bed that night.

Over the next weeks and months, established aspects of my behavior began to alter drastically before my own eyes. There was nothing self-willed about these changes, but I was nonetheless becoming someone I didn't know. The first thing to go was my sleep pattern, which I would previously have previously characterized as terrific. Quite overnight, I became a full-fledged insomniac. I lost interest in my teaching job (of fifteen years) and stopped socializing. Now afraid to compromise the privacy of people I cared about, I all but ignored my phone and rarely returned calls. One by one, my friends, professional associates, and family members were losing

Halt in Woodbridge

contact with me. I'm sure some took it personally. I made no attempt to clarify. Every new estrangement created another void in my life, and each void was gobbled up by the black hole of Bentwaters. Larry and I didn't speak again for a week. Though it had obviously never been his intention to cause me any harm or grief, he had in fact brought me into something well out of either of our control, and it was now catching up with both of us. Not that I disagreed with his method; had our situations been reversed, I'd never have told a potential collaborator everything up front." (*LAEG,* pages 286-287)

He contacts me – Larry Fawcett does – and I said "Well, I'll help you with the book if you keep it honest and straight forward and stick with the facts. We signed an agreement. I sent them off. Well, they lost interest in that book, etc. etc.

Despite the Machiavellian obstacle course we are soon to depart, Warren's relationship with Barry and Larry did give them important information that no one else had. Would two smart, dedicated and knowledgeable guys like them decide after all this to include Warren's 'lying account' in their book or even a reference to it once they were 'on to him?' Of course not. Why then, in terms of placement and inclusion, *is* Larry Warren's account not only included, but in effect, *as* the 'crown Jewel' in *Clear Intent?* The book's narrative builds to only one thing. The account of the airman known as 'Art Wallace.' There isn't a hint or expression of doubt on the part of either author, and the RFI portion of *Clear Intent* (pages 214-219) both open and close in a serious, respectful manner:

> "...when such stories are circulated in the media, a potential witness could be frightened away from reporting a UFO encounter. The threat of a fine and prison term for exposing the public to some yet unknown peril may be impetus enough to remain silent. One witness involved in the following encounter had precisely this fear in mind when he came forward to tell us what he had gone through. Persistent stories had come out of England about an unidentified

flying object which had come down into the Rendlesham Forest near the American Air Force Base at Bentwaters..."

Regarding Charles's offer of help "with Fawcett and Greenwood's book if they kept "...it honest and straight forward and stick with the facts." The colonel remained in the service until 1991 and as such would have had to move Air Force mountains in order to receive permission to become involved in such a commercial and potential embarrassing venture, embarrassing for the Air Force, that is. There is no reference to Charles Halt in this book other than the text of his memo (page 218). This paragraph immediately follows the one above:

> "Outside of some small variation in detail, the story in the document is amazingly similar to what Art Wallace described. This letter was certainly part of a more detailed file, since it is clear that an official investigation *was* conducted. ..." [3]

---

[3] *Clear Intent* was published by Prentice Hall Press in 1984, then republished by Fireside Books (a subsidiary of Simon & Schuster) in 1992 under the new title of *The UFO Cover-Up*.

Chapter 3:
Charles, Larry, and Peter

Then I get a call from Larry Warren and he's working with Peter Robbins. So I said "Larry, you weren't there. I sincerely believe he wasn't there. Now, and I've been telling him that for a long time. (Unclear)…document put them on a Flight. Now what probably happened, and I can only guess at this, he should have had five weeks of training after he got there, mandatory before you go on Flight. If we put someone on Flight that didn't have all the training, then the wing commander would have serious problems on this. It was serious, but, half a dozen cops. He's heard about it. So, did they put him on flight? I can't say he was or wasn't. He could have been in the forest. If he was in the forest, he would have done the (unclear) route (inaudible) back to the forest road and not probably close enough to see much of anything except by the radio (shack?). That's what I think, but I don't know that for a fact.

To characterize the above in two parts: upon learning that I had agreed to co-author a book with Larry, Halt repeatedly tells him that he (Larry) was not there – 'there' being out in the forest or farmer's field on the third night of UFO activity. He informs us that he has been telling Larry that he was not there "for a long time," this despite his own doubts about being correct. He concedes however if Larry *was* in the forest that night he "probably" would not have been close enough to see much of anything – this based on not knowing Larry's location at the time. That is what the colonel thinks or guesses, but doesn't know for a fact. There is no question here, only a contradictory stream of consciousness driven by an opinion based on a belief that he says he is unsure of. If you click on the link below it will take you to an episode of the radio show, "Behind the Paranormal With Paul and Ben Eno" The program was broadcast

Chapter 3: Charles, Larry, and Peter

on 11 April 2010, one of a series of 'Rendlesham Roundtables' the father-son broadcasting team managed to produce in the months leading up to the thirtieth anniversary of the RFI. This program was aired on CBS Radio in three cities: Detroit on WOMC 104.3 HD3, Boston on WBMX 104.1 HD3, and Seattle on KMPS 94.1 HD3. This particular Rendlesham Roundtable included Larry, Nick Pope, John Burroughs, Charles Halt, myself, and one or two other participants.[4]

In his talk, Charles acknowledges that a document shows that Larry had been put on a 'Flight,' then backtracks, asking "did they put him on Flight? I can't say he was or wasn't." This after saying they did. FYI the word 'Flight' in this context is a designated term for the particular Security Police unit, as in 'A Flight,' 'B Flight,' etc. Larry was assigned to and served with D Flight. The audience is then told that under normal circumstances Warren and other new SPs would have undergone a five week (at other times noted as a six or eight week) training period before actually becoming a Flight member. But this does not seem to have been the case for Larry. The simple fact was that his clearance came through on 15 December by which time

Larry Warren's Security Police Academy graduation photo. Taken during the summer of 1980 at Lackland Air Force Base, Texas. Warren appears second row, fourth from the left.

---

[4]If you listen to it you will hear the colonel acknowledge that Larry was there on the third night. http://www.behindtheparanormal.com/specialshows/rendlesham.html

Halt in Woodbridge

he'd finished his *two* weeks of incoming classes, and took his post while continuing his on the job training.

Security Police Academy Certificate of Training granted to AIC Lawrence P. Warren 28 October 1980.

In the spring of 1992, I learned through a colleague that the now-retired Deputy Base Commander of RAF Bentwaters wanted to speak with me. He had even given my friend his phone number with an invitation for me to call. While fully aware of the colonel's publicly stated doubts about Larry, I had wanted to speak with him for years. How could I not? Larry and I were almost five years into *Left At East Gate* and I wanted to interview the colonel. Wherever it might take us. And so on the afternoon of 23 June I laid out copies of Larry's Air Force paperwork on the desk in front of me, reviewed them one final time, then dialed the phone number. This was how my first conversation with Charles Halt began:

CH: Hello

PR: Mr. Halt?

CH: Yes.

PR: This is Peter Robbins, calling from New York,

CH: Oh, Peter Robbins! How are you? I've been looking forward to talking to you.

PR: Same with me. Did I pick a good time to call?

Chapter 3: Charles, Larry, and Peter

CH: Okay. That's fine. I can talk for about ten minutes or so.

PR: How long have you been retired sir?

CH: About a year.

PR: Is it alright with you if I record this?

CH: Go ahead.

PR: I know that the men who were involved are countering each other's accounts, and you've been very outspoken about what Larry says his participation was in that, and I just wanted…

CH: His participation *wasn't*.

PR: Why do you say that?

CH: Because he didn't come on duty until the middle of January, and I can show you documentation to prove that.

PR: Well, obviously I'd like to see it, I'm sitting here with some of his service record in front of me.

CH: Oh, you got his service record, good. Where did you find them? I'm curious.

PR: We're going to publish that. I actually can't say right now, although he did leave the service with some of his records. He actually left…

CH: I guess the question I'm asking you, did you get something from St. Louis?

PR: No.

CH: Okay. The question I'm asking you because it has a bearing on other things I might tell you or say.

PR: Fair enough.

CH: I'm not playing a game with you. I'll be very up front.

PR: I appreciate it. One of the things here is his assignment to D Flight, 2 December 1980.

CH: That's probably correct. When did he arrive at Bentwaters?

PR: Shortly before that.

CH: Okay. Now let me tell you this. There's a six to eight week training period where one doesn't not get a radio, a gun, a posting,

37

or anything 'til one has finished *all* of the training. Would you believe that?

PR: Well, I have...

CH: And I can provide a hundred witness can tell you that, including his supervisor, who I've just talked to, numerous times.

PR: Who was his supervisor?

CH: I'm not going to mention because he requested not to be identified.

PR: What I notice here is the indication at the bottom in Lee Swain's handwriting, "Airman Warren will be posted to duty roster, 'D' Flight, ten December 1980. Intro training will commence 5-12-80." And you're saying that training would have gone on into January?

CH: Six to eight weeks.

PR: Um hum.

CH: And I can assure you, as the deputy base commander, no cop picked up a weapon, picked up a radio, or was given a post until they completed training. I *guarantee* you. NATO came in and evaluated and looked at the records, the whole works. And we *knew* that up front. That was an ongoing thing.

PR: Well...

CH: What I'm trying to tell you is he's a fraud.

PR: *Well..*

CH: I don't think he knows he is. (*LAEG,* pages 324-325. Full transcript of June 25 1992 conversation, pages 324-334)

Larry arrived at my apartment two days later for our monthly work weekend. I played him the recording I'd made, then called Halt for the second time in two days. My intention to initiate a conversation between Larry and Charles. Before handing over the phone to Larry the colonel and I had this brief exchange:

PR: I asked you several times if there was *any* chance Larry had gotten his PRP (that is, completed his Personal Recognisance

Chapter 3: Charles, Larry, and Peter

Program) by 15 December or so and you said absolutely not. But if we could establish for you, on your own terms, with official Air Force documentation, that he had been assigned to Flight by mid-December and was on Flight that night. If we could establish that for you, would you feel that, perhaps, there are other problems with...

CH: You show me the documents and then...

PR: Can Larry actually speak with you about the documents we have here?

CH: I'd rather see them, because I've seen other documents that he was assigned later. Something's wrong.

PR: Well what I'm asking is this, will you speak to Larry on this point right now?

CH: Sure.

(*LAEG*, page 335. Full transcript of June 25 1992 conversation, pages 334-340)

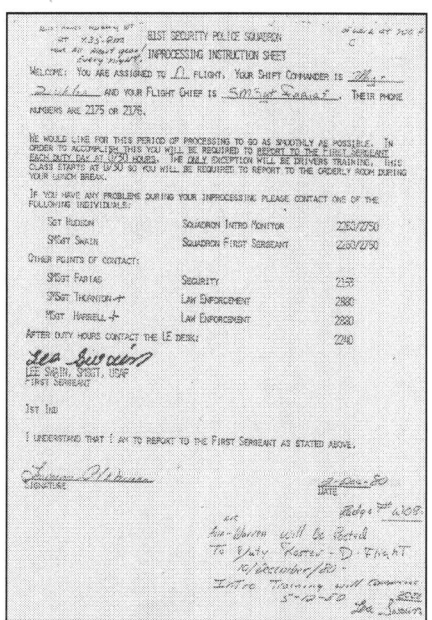

Airman Warren's 2 December 1980 SPS
Inprocessing Sheet.

Halt in Woodbridge

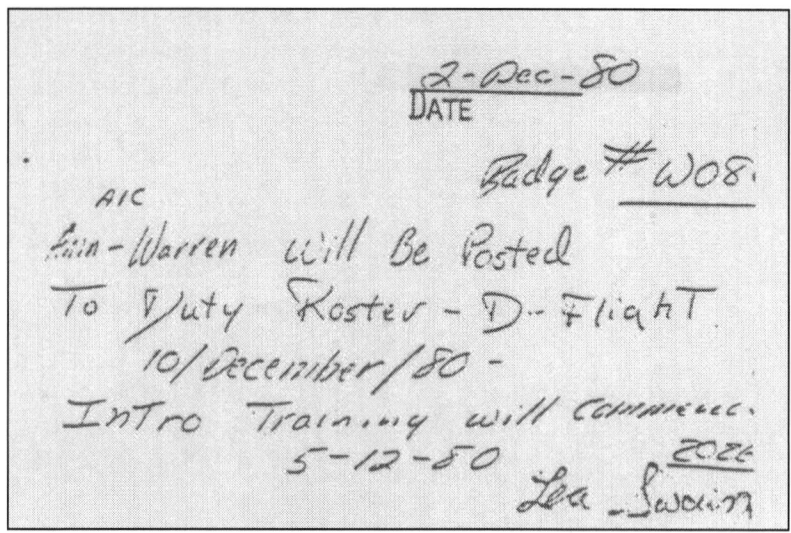

Close-up from Warren's 2 December 1980 Inprocessing Sheet.

Seven months later, on Tuesday 16 February 1993 at 1:30 in the afternoon to be precise, Charles Halt, Larry Warren, myself, and Bob Oeschler, a Maryland-based UFO researcher who was kind enough to drive us to our meeting. We met in the food court of a shopping mall appropriately named Pentagon City, just across the highway from the massive headquarters of the United States military. We found an empty table and talked for more than an hour. I recorded our conversation while Bob made a back-up copy just in case. The choice of time and place were the colonel's and Larry, Bob and I all noticed that every once in a while Mr. Halt would look up into one of the balconied areas, always at the same spot and at who we could only guess. Anyone with a serious interest in the RFI owes it to themselves to read this transcript. It's insightful, unnerving, and at times fairly moving. The colonel had told us he had documents that established Larry could not have been posted to the SPs at the time of the event, thus proving he could not have involved in the RFI. This is evinced by the following February 1993 exchange:

> PR: I do want to ask you though, do you feel that there is any chance that *you* have been misled as to Larry's involvement.

Chapter 3: Charles, Larry, and Peter

CH: No, I don't think so. I will tell you this, if you publish the book with disinformation, I'm going to go back to the publisher and I will make some noise about it, 'cause there's... I think you're being used. Honestly I do, and I'm just going to tell you that right now. For what it's worth.

PR: Um Hum, Well, it certainly not the first time I've heard it.

CH: No. I have talked to enough of the players that are far enough removed on the peripheral, who knew who was involved and who knew enough about it to know there's some funny things afoot.

PR: Would you be willing to sit down with Larry *and* me, in Washington, if we can get down there...

CH: Sure, come on down.

PR: ...and run through this stuff, and present it (the documents he was referring to) to *us*, as opposed to just me?

CH: Sure.

PR: Fair enough.

CH: Now, I don't have all the documents right here at my house, and I'm waiting for some to come.

PR: Okay. I think we should plan to take you up on that, and it certainly won't be...

CH: I'd recommend it before you publish the book. It will save some embarrassment in professional circles for you. I mean that's just a recommendation.

PR: No, I hear you.

The above understood, several minutes into our Pentagon City conversation, there was this exchange between Warren and Halt:

LW: I never wanted to embarrass or hurt anybody.

CH: I don't accuse anybody of that, other than some of the press and a few loonies in England. Do you remember two separate distinct nights or were you involved in one night? [Larry indicates one] do you have the 2095 assigning you to Flight?

LW: Yes.

CH: Why don't you show me what you have?

Halt and Warren review his 2095, the above letter from Major Zickler, 2 December 1980 Inprocessing Sheet and U.K. whip sheets.

LW: That's a copy, we have the original of that file. I had PRP (Personal Recognisance Program) instantly when I was there. I got posted on the eleventh or the fifteenth. Of course, OJT (On the Job Training) continues throughout your career, so there's a lot of courses I never even got to take. [Indicating document] I was certified on 15 December.

Larry explains to Charles the terms under which he'd left the service, that being the Air Force's having been in breach of contract when they took him off SP duties and reassigned him to office duties. Larry also told Charles about his meeting with base lawyer Major Persky who agreed that this had been the case:

LW: And he said, you can get out, honorable discharge, and then go back to the States.

CH: Did you actually initiate the request?

LW: Oh yes, absolutely. I wasn't doing my job, and I was worried about a few things going on. I want you to notice here, Non-fulfillment of guaranteed enlistee training." When I got out, I went to my old recruiter, and all of a sudden up on the computer it said, "Do not process. Nothing follows." I got in touch with my congressman at the time, got in touch with the Department of the Air Force trying to find something out..."

(*LAEG*, pages 356-357. Full transcript of the conversation, pages 352-366)

Make no mistake. On February 16 1993 Charles Halt personally reviewed copies of the above referenced documents for himself. He didn't question their authenticity in any way. And the documents he had that proved Larry wrong? We never saw them. In comparing notes after the fact both Larry and I felt a little embarrassed for the colonel. That's why neither of us challenged him on this. In retrospect I wish we had. Did Halt even have the documents with him? Did they even exist? Had he been bluffing? Had he come to realize while examining Larry's papers that it was *his* documents that were in some way inauthentic and not Warren's? I don't expect we'll ever know the answer to that question. But there is no question that he was not telling the truth in Woodbridge when he said "did they put him on Flight? I can't say he was or wasn't." The colonel knew for a fact that Warren had been posted to D Flight that night. He knew it twenty-two years ago.

Halt in Woodbridge

> ON OR ABOUT 12-1-80
>
> DEPARTMENT OF THE AIR FORCE
> 81ST SECURITY POLICE SQUADRON (USAFE)
> APO NEW YORK 09755
>
> AB Lawrence P. Warren
> 3280 Technical Training Gp
> Lackland AFB TX 78236
>
> Dear Lawrence,
>
> Welcome to RAF Bentwaters/Woodbridge and the 81st Security Police Squadron. We are looking forward to your arrival and your help in maintaining the 81st's reputation as the best security police squadron in USAFE.
>
> I have asked Amn James C. Gouge to be your sponsor. He knows the squadron and can answer your questions about England. His address is Box 3189, APO New York 09755. I have given a package of brochures on England and the bases to Amn Gouge. He will send them to you with his letter. Please use your sponsor, to answer your questions and make your move easier.
>
> Most of our single airmen live in modern dorms on Bentwaters where they are close to the services and conveniences of the base. If you want to live off base, you must process through the base housing referral office prior to making any commitments. Single BAQ is only paid to single airmen living off base when dormitory space is not available, an unusual situation, and one that fluctuates with squadron composition and size. Off base housing is limited, hard to find, expensive, and not built to the standards most Americans would expect.
>
> Sgt Dennis K. Hudson is in charge of our sponsorship program. Because of our shift work he will probably meet you and get you settled the first day or two before you meet Amn Gouge. Sgt Hudson works 8 to 5, Mon thru Fri, and can be reached at AUTOVON 225-2750/2260.
>
> Again, welcome. Have a pleasant trip and I'll meet you when you arrive. Your tour in the United Kingdom will be rewarding I'm sure.
>
> Sincerely,
>
> /S/
>
> MALCOLM S. ZICKLER, Major, USAF
> Commander

Maj. Malcolm S. Zickler's 1 December 1980 'Welcome to RAF Bentwaters/Woodbridge letter. The major was the Commander of the 81st Security Police Squadron that Larry Warren served with.

Chapter 4:

The Colonel vs. *Left At East Gate*

For those of you who have read *Left At East Gate*, I'd like to give you some updates and some potential corrections that Mr. Warren and his co-author can put into their next book.

Thank you Charles. For readers with copies of *Left At East Gate,* either edition will do. The paging is identical in both the 1997 and 2005 versions. The added pages in the newer version are set off in Roman numerals. To the colonel's "potential corrections:"

If you take the original version and you go to page 32, he claims we had a "Helping Hand. We had no Helping Hands. Helping Hands were very serious (unclear) report (unclear). Everybody in the base would know about it. Trust me.

Larry Warren not only "claims" there was a Helping Hand, he was the one who initiated it. I was surprised the colonel failed to mention this until I read the circumstances leading up to it. Initiating the Air Force procedure known as "Helping Hand" is very serious indeed. Pages 226-227 of the February 1979 edition of USAF *Basic Security Specialist Course* manual defines it as, "an unclassified telephone message transmitted rapidly up the channel of command to inform appropriate higher headquarters that a possibly hostile event that could affect the ready general war capability has been detected at the base or at a dispersed site. It applied to priority "A" or "B" resources and to bases possessing or supporting such resources. The HELPING HAND report, a brief description of the event that prompted the report, is transmitted up the communications channels of the major command securing the resources involved. The primary command control communications of the major command will be used in all possible instances; otherwise, secondary communication linkages, or, as a last resort, commercial telephone will be used."

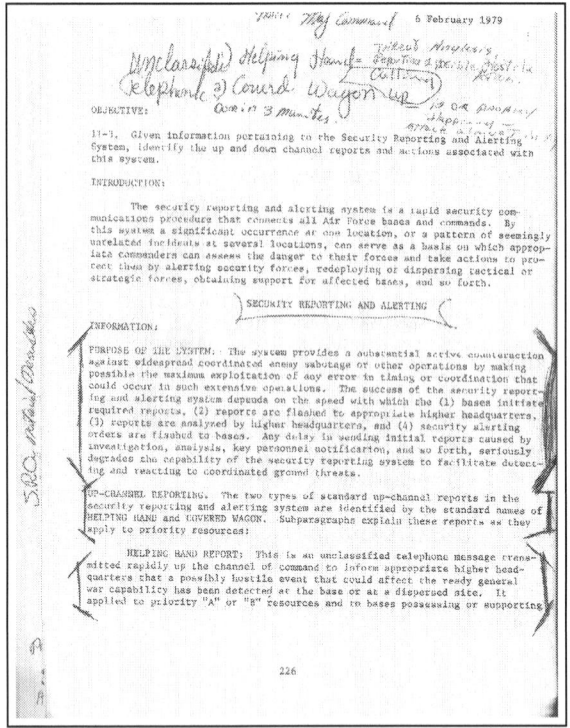

From Larry Warren's copy of Basic Security Specialist Course manual, page 226.

Warren understood the seriousness of initiating such a report. It's referenced in the handwritten notes he made in his copy of the manual. This the event that triggered Security Specialist Warren's calling in a Helping Hand:

"One incident that week I won't forget. One night, just before our first three-day break, which extended over the Christmas holiday, a few other SPs and I were assigned to an active aircraft area on the Bentwaters flight line. About half way into the shift, we realized someone was shooting at us. They were firing from the woods just beyond the perimeter fence. The bullets seemed to be from a small calibre weapon. We knew this because the report wasn't very loud. However, bullets are bullets. I hit the ground when a few bullets struck an A-10 (aircraft) not far from my position. The aircraft were loaded with active bombs because they were due to go on training runs in Norfolk the next morning, making the situation even graver.

I called central security control and reported a Helping Hand – a procedure aptly named! Out on the tarmac, a fellow SP named Russ was low-crawling and calling out on his handheld Motorola that the Vietcong were on the wire! He had to be restrained because we were not allowed to return fire off base, due to the treaty with Britain. After about fifteen minutes, whoever had done the shooting was gone. The weapon turned out to be a 22-calibre rifle. Damage assessment showed that only two rounds had hit the A-10, no more than scratching its titanium surface. Russ was eventually snapped out and put under observation, I never worked with him again."

Did Larry's making this report meet the protocols for a Helping Hand as defined in the *Security Specialist Course* manual? Definitely. Did he act to "inform appropriate higher headquarters that a possibly hostile event that could affect the ready general war capability has been detected at the base or at a dispersed site"? Without question. Charles says "We had no Helping Hands." Ever? Or just that he was aware of, or is it something he may have forgotten after almost thirty five years? I have no way of knowing if "Everybody in the base" learned of this event, but I'm damned sure the SPs involved and likely then some would have. But why mention the Helping Hand, and the 'fact' that it never happened while excluding any reference to Warren's account of the circumstances that initiated it? Let the reader draw their own conclusions. (*LAEG*, pages 31 and 32)

If you go to page 39, he said the base was on alert. The base was not on alert. We were at a party. A social event. There was no alert.

"The base was not on alert. We were at a party." Really? Despite the fact that the colonel and other officers and their

Halt in Woodbridge

wives were enjoying a late Christmas/early New Years party that evening, a potential military crisis was coming to a head in Eastern Europe leaving the NATO establishment in anything but a party mood. You've only to consult the front page or international section of any major newspaper for that week to understand why. This is how Larry described the situation as he was preparing to go on duty on what was to be the third and final night of the Rendlesham Forest UFO incident:

> "I was back in my dorm around eight, got my uniform ready, and grabbed my alert bag, containing a flack vest, chemical suit, and other equipment. The base was on alert at that time because the Soviet Union was on the brink of moving armored units into Poland to stop the solidarity movement and the general unrest it had sparked. NATO forces were ready to respond if the Red Army crossed the line. Most of our A-10 tank busters had already left for forward operating locations in West Germany the previous week; very few aircraft remained at Bentwaters. This was a tense time in Europe, though we didn't feel war was imminent." (*LAEG,* page 40)

RAF Bentwaters was most definitely on alert that night, as were other NATO bases throughout the United Kingdom and Europe.

Page 39 - He shows a picture in the book of an alert sign alert status but he cuts off the top, and he cuts off the bottom part because we have sliding things that says where the alert is, but you can't see that. He's got sandbags up.

Take a moment to study the photo Charles refers to here. Larry took this picture on the very morning of the third night's UFO event which like the rest of the RFI took place during the Polish crisis. Larry had a new instamatic camera with him and was running a first roll of film through it, as we used to do back in the pre-digital days. "He cuts off the top"? What is he talking about? As you can see, *nothing* is cut off the top of this sign and there is no way whatsoever to interpret it as such. The audience

Chapter 4: The Colonel vs. Left at East Gate

Alert sign at Main Gate of RAF Bentwaters, late December 1980. Photo: Larry Warren.

is then told, "he cuts off the bottom part because we have sliding things that says where the alert is, but you can't see that. *He's got sandbags up*" (emphasis mine). Larry "cut off" nothing. He simply took a snapshot of the sign as it appeared at that time. No effort was made to 'hide' the lower part, and to suggest that Warren did so intentionally to block "the sliding thing" that may have indicated the location of the alert? What would it have said? Poland? This accusation is really stretching things but the last charge is the most ludicrous: "He's (Larry's) got sandbags up:" Shame on you Airman Warren for piling up those sandbags and intentionally block the sliding thing. Forgive the momentary levity, but all of the above charges are absurd.

Halt in Woodbridge

Alert condition, December 1981 – condition normal, May 1981. Graphic: Dave Kelly.

I've got pictures, but I don't have time to put all that up for you. You won't get done tonight.

Pictures of what? And in what manner do they bear on the above or anything else, and where are they? If the pictures had been part of his PowerPoint the audience would have seen them projected on the screen. He obviously chose not to include them though he'd had months to prepare the visuals that would accompany his talk. The audience never learns the answers to these questions because Charles 'did not have time to show them.' In fact he did have the time to do so. The event concluded about half an hour early before it was scheduled to. I know the colonel is seventy-five years old and understand he may have been tired as he'd taken others on a walk in the Rendlesham

50

Chapter 4: The Colonel vs. Left at East Gate

Forest earlier, but he did have the time.

If you go to page 42 he claims that we had his captain at the motor pool. There was no captain at the motor pool. There were two Security Police captains. Captain (unclear) and Captain Verrano. Guess where they were at? They were at the party.

Were the SPS captains at the party? Sure, why not, but if they were, at some point following Col. Halt's departure, they would have inevitably left as well. The only voice that really matters here is 81st SPS Captain Mike Verrano's. This is some of what he wrote to Larry in 1997 after reading *Left At East Gate*. Aside from verifying his presence at the motor pool, it confirms other important information about another of the other officers involved:

> "I was at the motor pool because no O Level was available that night. I was on call, other command people were busy elsewhere, maybe on sight? I remember the malfunctions with the lightalls very well. Do you recall the vehicle malfunctions? I did drive Williams (Colonel Gordon Williams, RAF Bentwaters Wing Commander) to an F-16 on the Bentwaters tarmac the AM of the 30th. He had two canisters of 35 mm footage with him, bagged in a T.S. [Top Secret] satchel. He told me directly that it was actual footage of the UFOs etc on the ground. That film was shot on your night in the forest. The film went to USAFE, West Germany that day and I never heard its deposition after that." (*LAEG*, 2005 Cosimo Books edition, pages xxv-xxvi)

If you go to page 33 & 34, British police were present. I have two British constabulary who established exactly what was in the (inaudible) what they (inaudible) and what (where?) they were. They responded twice. The first night after everything was over they came out, and it was too late, they found nothing. They came out the next afternoon, found indentations and said, "Well, looks like scratching of a rabbit

or whatever." That's the only two times, and says very clearly at the bottom, which I am going to give to somebody tonight when I leave. That they only responded during that period two times. They had a serious burglary in the post office and they had a lot of things, but they did not respond other than that

There is no reference whatsoever to the two British police officers on either page 33 or 34. It appears on page 46. Errors of this basic nature suggest that factual references do not mean that much to Mr. Halt, a general approximation being good enough. This is what Warren actually observed:

> "Some of the people who had run off into the woods were called back. I could see their faces in the distance, but they held their ground. To my right were two English policemen from the town of Woodbridge. One had a camera and was snapping pictures. An airman was ordered to take it away; he did so forcefully and an argument ensued. By now, the level of tension had increased twofold."

Adrian Bustinza remembers them in his April 1984 interview with Larry Fawcett:

> LF. Okay. From that point you went into the woods in a line I guess. Were there any bobbies there or British police or anything?
>
> AB. Not at the beginning.
>
> LF. Not at the beginning?
>
> AB. No.

We know that one of the bobbies in the field on the third night is named Brian Cresswell and he may still live in the Woodbridge area if anyone is interested. But again, we need to see the colonel's letters and learn what their provenance is.

If you turn to page 44 there were 'hot spots.' We had them roped off with surveyor's tape. We don't need surveyor's tape. 40 people were out there. Originally it was 200, then it

Chapter 4: The Colonel vs. Left at East Gate

was 40. At the most, counting us, there were 25.

The colonel's numbers here are confusing, but this is what Larry wrote about the above in *Left At East Gate:*

"After roughly one hundred yards, we turned right and continued deeper into the forest. The pines were very dense at this point. Off to my left, I could see an area illuminated by large flashlights and a ground flare or two. I could see silhouettes of people moving around that area. I also noticed what looked like orange or red surveyor's tape wrapped around some trees. The lighting effect was eerie. My mind was still processing information, unimpaired.

Then I heard a radio transmission, "You people have to avoid those hot spots. Remember they're marked, October November One. Over" I knew the code "October One" meant first officer on site. What "hot spot meant" I didn't know. Maybe we were going to fight a forest fire, but why us? We were cops, not firemen."

Whether or not surveyor's tape was needed, that is what Larry observed, despite Halt's opinion to the contrary. Then again, perhaps Warren invented this relatively minor detail, then decided to throw it into the mix for whatever reason – or that it was a deliberately planted false memory. While the colonel does not deny the presence of said hot spots he points to something more interesting, to me in any case. There were two hundred personnel out there that night? Then there were forty, then twenty-five? Out *where* precisely? In the 'hot spot' area? In and around the logging road? Generally spread out through that part of the forest? More significantly, why had two hundred United States Air Force personnel been ordered into an otherwise quiet, non-strategic area of forest and field that night to begin with?

Page 46, Gordon Williams drove by in his staff car and Don Moreland. Don Moreland was in Wales.

Halt specifically told the audience that Warren placed British Liaison Officer, Squadron Leader Donald Moreland, assigned to

Halt in Woodbridge

RAF Woodbridge at this time, at a specified location along with Col. Williams on the third night of UFO activity. He then in effect shows Warren to be wrong as Moreland could not have been present due to the fact he was in Wales; embarrassing stuff for Larry if true. But Charles is not only wrong, he is very wrong. There is no reference whatever to Squadron Leader Moreland on page 46, nor on page 45 or page 47. Moreland is referred to exactly three times in *Left At East Gate,* on pages 103, 107 and 329, but nowhere else other than its index. How does one account for such a glaring error? Halt gives a page number, places a person on it who never existed there, than tells his audience that this was the case – *and* that Warren is incorrect in what he wrote in placing Moreland there. How can such an 'error' be accidental?

(again, page 46): "The staff car could not have been driven down that road. We had troubles with the jeep, and he drove into the field? He'd have had to go over a big burn, a track vehicle, and over a barbed wire fence."

Col. Halt is absolutely correct in stating that Col. Williams' staff car – or any other vehicle, could not possibly have been driven all the way down the logging road and out into the field. But Warren has never stated or claimed any such thing. No matter. Earlier in the day Charles repeated this imaginary charge to others during a walk down the Rendlesham Forest logging road and out to the farmer's field known as Capel Green.

Chapter 5:
A Walk In the Forest

In 1980 we were up there a little ways – but, there's a barbed wire fence here and there's a burn here, and this nonsense about Gordon Williams coming out with the staff car, number one – he couldn't have gotten down to the road because it was a big American staff car with about that much (indicating) that much ground clearance. If he got about part way down he'd have had to be towed back. And the comments made, he went out into the field – he'd have had to drive through a barbed wire fence, over a burn, with a trapped vehicle to get over a big farm (unclear) there. There's a big burn there. So it's nonsense that he drove out into the field. He didn't come out. We know that.

Even while only a rustic utility road running through a forest, it's a *road,* and any vehicle –then or now, can easily make its way down toward the field *until that point where it becomes a trail*, then under-brush makes it impossible for a car or truck to go any further. At least a part of Charles's seeming problem is that he either misread, misremembered, or intentionally misrepresented the relevant passage. The exact words Warren used to describe this moment are these:

> "Suddenly, a staff car arrived at the end of the trail. Col. Gordon Williams and other staff officers got out and spoke with officers already on the site."

Nowhere does he say or suggest that the car made its way from the logging road onto the trail, then into Capel Green. The vehicle arrived at the end of the trail to the degree that it was drivable, and *then* "Col. Gordon Williams and other staff officers *got out* and spoke with officers already on the site." Can we put this baby to bed now?

Halt in Woodbridge

An unblocked view of Capel Green, winter 2014. Photo: Peter Robbins.

Let's remain in Capel Green a bit longer. On Saturday afternoon 11 July the colonel, accompanied by event organizers Hanson and Bryant and perhaps twenty others took the walk described with Halt giving a running commentary as they went. Ben Emlyn-Jones, an Oxford-based radio programme host, accompanied the group. He had come to Woodbridge at the request of John Hanson to record the conference, also recorded the walk in the forest, until Charles asked him to turn off his camera. Emlyn-Jones:

> "Despite Bryant's claims that I "infiltrated" the event, I made my film according to John's instructions. He knows my opinions on Larry's story and brought me into the project in full knowledge of that. He trusted me to make a professional film and I delivered."

Ben's feeling is that Bryant's protests were made to keep the public from seeing what he had filmed, and with good cause I think. Some of the forest footage portrays a figure in authority saying things that are simply untrue but generally accepted by those listening because they know no better. And in the process Charles again undermines the credibility and reputation of someone who was not there to defend himself against completely incorrect allegations.

...there were no hedgerows you could see all the windows

Chapter 5: A Walk in the Forest

and the farmhouse was as dark as could be. And I was concerned and I thought two things: their safety, number one, with what was going on. And number two that they would find us and call the police or the authorities, but the lights never came on in the farmhouse despite what it says in East at the Guest Hate – East Gate, or whatever.

This bit of whimsy notwithstanding, Halt is referring to a two-part observation that Warren made in the minutes leading up to the actual encounter. First this:

"Bustinza pointed to a farm house about two hundred yards away. I could see a light on in an upper-floor window. I briefly wondered if the home's occupants could see what I was seeing." (*LAEG*, page 45)

A view of Capel Green with the farmhouse to the left. Photo: Peter Robbins.

Warren and Halt observe the farmhouse from different vantage points at different times. Isn't it just possible, even likely, that somewhere between their separate observations one of the residents was either awakened by the military contingent in the field or for some other conventional reason, then turned on a light in their bedroom? In essence what the colonel is saying is, because the house was dark when *he* observed it, a second floor light could not have been on when Warren observed it, and that this 'logic' establishes that Larry was fabricating what he reported. This would almost be funny if it weren't so insulting to one's intelligence.

There were no cattle in the field either, which is stated. The cattle were in a barn. We did see evidence cattle had been in the field because somebody stepped in one of the piles. We were out looking for any residue that came off the object.

Larry Warren:

> "We joined the forty-odd other men already in the field, just looking at the bizarre object on the ground in front of us. Two cows walked out of the dark to my left. They looked dazed, but none of the human activity seemed to phase them I asked: "Where did they come from?" (*LAEG,* page 45)

If a tree falls in the forest and no one sees it, does it still make a sound? This maxim applies to both of these charges, silly though they may be. There is no way Halt could have known if all of the farmer's cattle were in the barn. More, in this case he presents us with the very evidence necessary to negate his charge. It's clear from his statement that at least one cow had been in the vicinity, and recently enough that one of Halt's men stepped in fresh cow "evidence" at that location. Is it much of a stretch to assume that the cow or cows responsible had come and gone, but that their visits were not synchronized with those of the colonel and his men? Attempting to cite these incidents as 'evidence' of Warren's dubious relationship with the truth only reflects poorly on the colonel's relationship with same.

There's certainly a possibility that Larry Warren was there. He shouldn't have been there. Let me explain why. He came on the base in mid-December. There's a mandatory 5 week

training period before you are allowed to pick up a weapon for the clearance which you need to do. He had not completed that. They had a document with the right name on it that he was put on duty sometime around the twenty-third or twenty-forth or something. Maybe he could. He may have been out here and I didn't know it, but if he was out here he never left that area (pointing to the left) because they were given a direct order not to leave there.

Despite this matter's having been fully settled some twenty three years earlier and *in person*, the colonel is still unable to keep himself from promulgating this absolute falsehood. And on the night in question Security Specialist Warren's orders were to indeed to 'leave the area' with the other men and head into the forest in the direction of Capel Green.

There were no British RAF people here. The only RAF guy for miles was Don Moreland and he was in Wales on vacation for the holidays. That's why my memo stated ten days or twelve days later because I had to wait for him to come back. So all that nonsense about film crews and tripods and police everywhere, confiscating films and cameras

DAVID BRYANT [mocking chuckle]: it's a good story.[5]

It is a good story, but it's the colonel's story, not Warren's. Nowhere in our book or in any other written or spoken form has Larry Warren stated or suggested that there were any "British RAF people" or other British military personnel present at this time. Nor has he ever stated, suggested or written that Donald Moreland was present either. The same goes for "Police everywhere," as only two were briefly on location, and only one of them – singular – had a camera involving only one roll of

---

[5] I hope readers will view the recording for themselves to see and hear if I'm mischaracterizing this or anything else.

Halt in Woodbridge

confiscated film. Halt's exaggerations do not do a service for the facts. (*LAEG*, page 46)

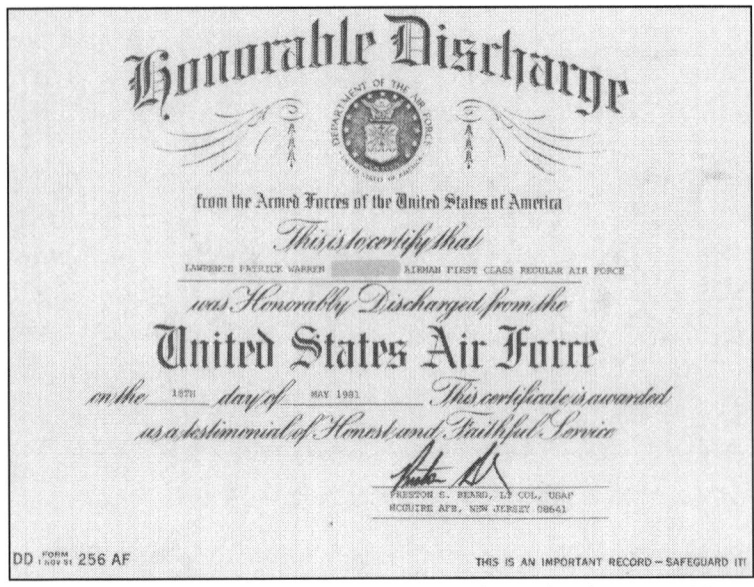

A copy of Larry Warren's (fully) Honorable Discharge dated 18 May 1981.

DAVID BRYANT: You know how Warren is fond of waving about this honorable discharge? I am right in thinking it's just something you get? (chuckles)

CH: Let me explain something. A 39/10 Discharge. Do you know what a 39/10 is? It's suitability/undesirability. Leave for the convenience of the service. I'm serious. (BRYANT laughs out loudly)

BRYANT: It makes a lot of sense.

David Bryant needs to understand that an honorable discharge from the United States Air Force is not just something you *get*, and Charles Halt needs to take responsibility for misrepresenting the nature of the discharge Larry Warren received. And shame on him for not coming to the defense of the Air Force Honorable

Chapter 5: A Walk in the Forest

Discharge. Mr. Halt knows the words "Honorably Discharged" actually stand for something despite his characterization above. Charles asks those with him if they know what a 39/10 is, fully aware that these British citizens will not have a clue. He then tells them something which is entirely untrue.

As was established in our face-to-face meeting with the colonel, Larry left the service with a highly classified 4-M discharge code (*LAEG* page 354) which Halt himself was and is not cleared to know the meaning of. A 39/10 is an Air Force *regulation* that is applied *only* in situations where the USAF is legally at fault for breach of contract and only then. In this case, the Air Force took Security Specialist Warren off his SP duties and assigned him to office work, thus breaking their contract with him. Carefully reread his 22 April 1981 'Request for Separation' form (below) and you'll see that his honorable discharge was granted for one reason and one reason only: "Nonfulfillment of Guaranteed Training Enlistee Program Agreement." In this case the phrase, "in the best interests of himself and the United States Air Force," puts the blame squarely on the service branch for breaking its contract with the Security Specialist and not the other way around. The colonel will go on to repeat these and other untruths to the paying crowd later that day.

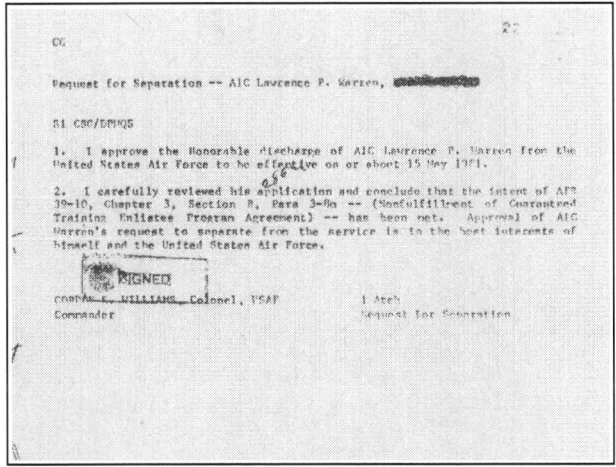

A second look at Larry Warren's 'Request for Separation' dated 22 April 1981.

Halt in Woodbridge

BEN EMLYN-JONES: He wrote a letter to his mum.

HALT: Oh yeah, he did. On sixth January. Based on what Adrian Bustinza, who was with me, went back to the dormitory – and I have this email – and it says, "The first guy I ran into was Larry Warren so I told him the whole story." (Reaction from the small crowd, a few 'knowing' 'Ohs') Then the other cops are talking and he picked up enough bits and pieces, and he put himself into the story. Peter Robbins knows all this! He has to – he's not a dumb guy.

BRYANT: (in a decidedly mocking tone) Of course he does!

BEN: But, as always ladies and gentleman, look at both sides of the story and make your own minds up. That's all I can say.

BEN: Colonel, what do you think when it comes to Larry. He had a medical report (in) which he was injured and he was suffering from bleeding skin.

HALT: You're not recording this are you?

BEN: I can switch it off.

Halt then asks for Ben to switch off his camera which Ben does.

Ipswich Evening Star's coverage of the significance of Warren's 6 January 1981 letter to his family. The article appeared in autumn 2014.

Chapter 6:
Anomalous Injuries

> BEN (voiceover): Colonel Halt told me what he believed was the cause of Larry Warren's injuries which he describes in *LAEG*... In doing so, Col Halt reiterates something he said on a radio show in December of last year. He believes that the injuries Larry sustained were a result of his alleged drug addiction.... There's just a little bit at about five minutes in. It's very unclear, but this is mostly what I could make out; Halt - off camera - also blamed drug abuse for Larry bleeding through his skin.

Charles Halt has accused Larry Warren of having been a "drug addict" on and off for years. Even given the extra-serious nature of such a charge, he again backs it up with nothing but a 'take my word for it.' Is this something Halt even believes to be true? No matter. I'm convinced its just one more thing he wants others to believe is true. What are the actual facts regarding the anomalous injuries suffered by Warren? And what, if anything, might connect them with the repeated use of illicit drugs as suggested by Col. Halt. Here is the first set of specifics for you to consider. Larry Warren:

> "Over the preceding year, I'd begun to have an unusual medical problem. The skin at the base of my neck and the top of my back would first start to get hot, then I would begin to bleed through the skin. It would happen without warning, and ruined a dozen shirts that year. Late one June night as Cindy and I sat watching TV, she suddenly moved back and said, "My God Larry, you're bleeding again." The back of my yellow t-shirt was already red. That was it for her: "We are going to the hospital," she said. Cindy was an occupational therapist at one of the hospitals in New Britain, Connecticut, and called their emergency room immediately. Cindy knew the nurse who answered and described the situation as best she could. The nurse expressed concern over the amount of blood I was losing and asked Cin to get me to the ER. I couldn't stop the

Halt in Woodbridge

bleeding and was getting weak. Once in the ER we waited to be seen by a doctor. When my turn came, I was shown into a small room and Cindy followed. She thought I had ruptured a blood vessel at the surface of my skin, and I hoped that was all it was. I hated hospitals and just wanted to get out of there.

A doctor entered the room and asked questions about the bleeding, such as how long had it been going on. I told him on and off for about a year. He took some blood and asked us to wait. He returned after about an hour and told us the tests were showing some strange things; he and some other doctors were going to do some more tests and again he asked

Though Cindy was concerned, I had now stopped the bleeding by applying direct pressure. After almost four hours, three doctors entered the room. The oldest of them said he had some questions for me and that I shouldn't be alarmed. "Were you in Vietnam?" he asked. I said "No, I was too young." "When you were in the service, did you work around any nuclear devices?" "Yes," I answered. "Larry," he said, "our tests show that you may have been exposed to an unshielded nuclear device. Can you recall any time that this might have happened?" Cindy's face dropped. "Yes," I answered, "but you wouldn't believe me if I told you." I was told that my white blood cells showed signs of having been heavily dosed by rads. One of the effects would be occasional hemorrhaging through the skin. All three doctors seemed puzzled; if I'd been so exposed, such effects shouldn't be showing up for twenty years or so. It had only been four years since Bentwaters. The doctors asked me to keep them posted on any further developments, then spoke with Cindy, telling her to keep an eye on me. Then we drove back home. I was scared. Were the other guys having health problems? Did the Air Force know they had brought us into a dangerous situation that night? Was I going to die because of it?" (*LAEG*, pages 126-127)

I wouldn't expect Charles Halt to take Larry's or my word for this, or even Cindy's. For me he is the embodiment of Stanton T. Friedman's perceptive maxim, "Don't bother me with the facts. My mind is already made up." The colonel knows what he believes and that is good enough for him. Or, he knows what he's supposed to make others believe and *that* is good enough

64

Chapter 6: Anomalous Injuries

for him. What follow are copies of the New Britain General Hospital emergency room treatment records that Larry and Cindy received following his 18 July 1984 emergency visit:

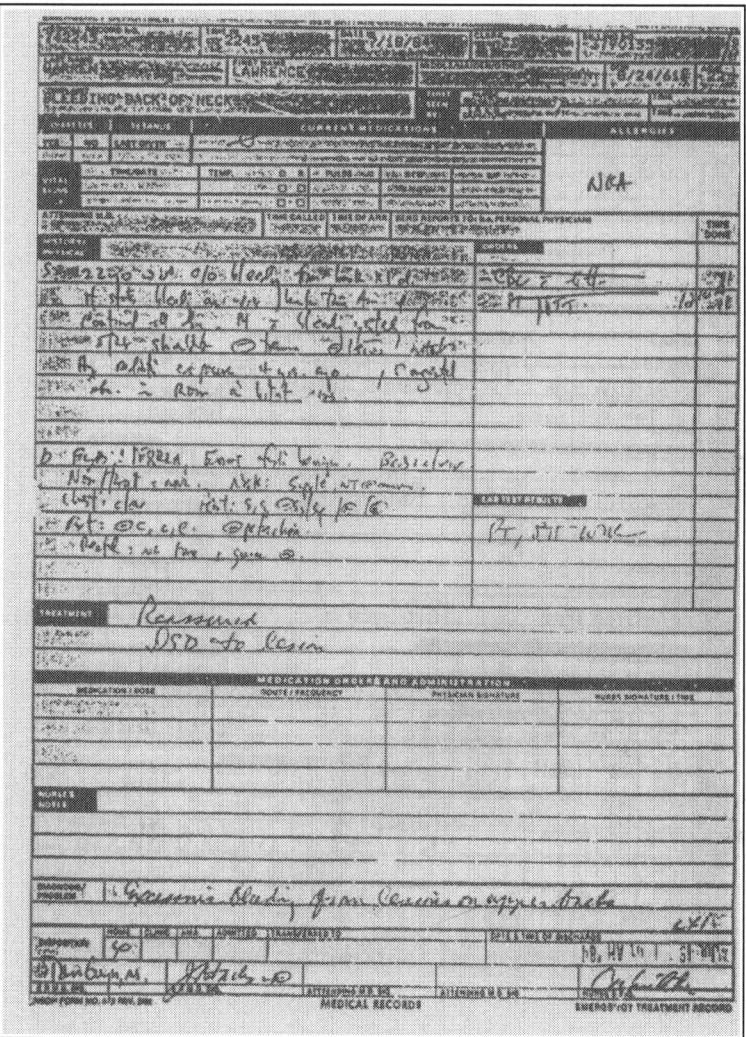

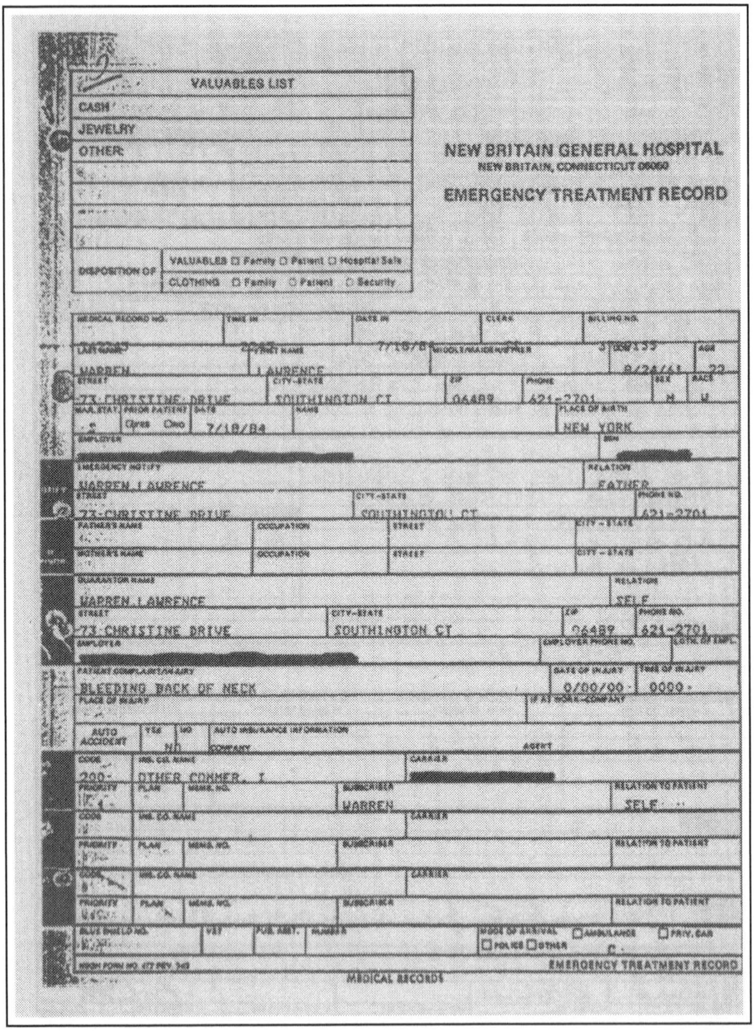

Chapter 6: Anomalous Injuries

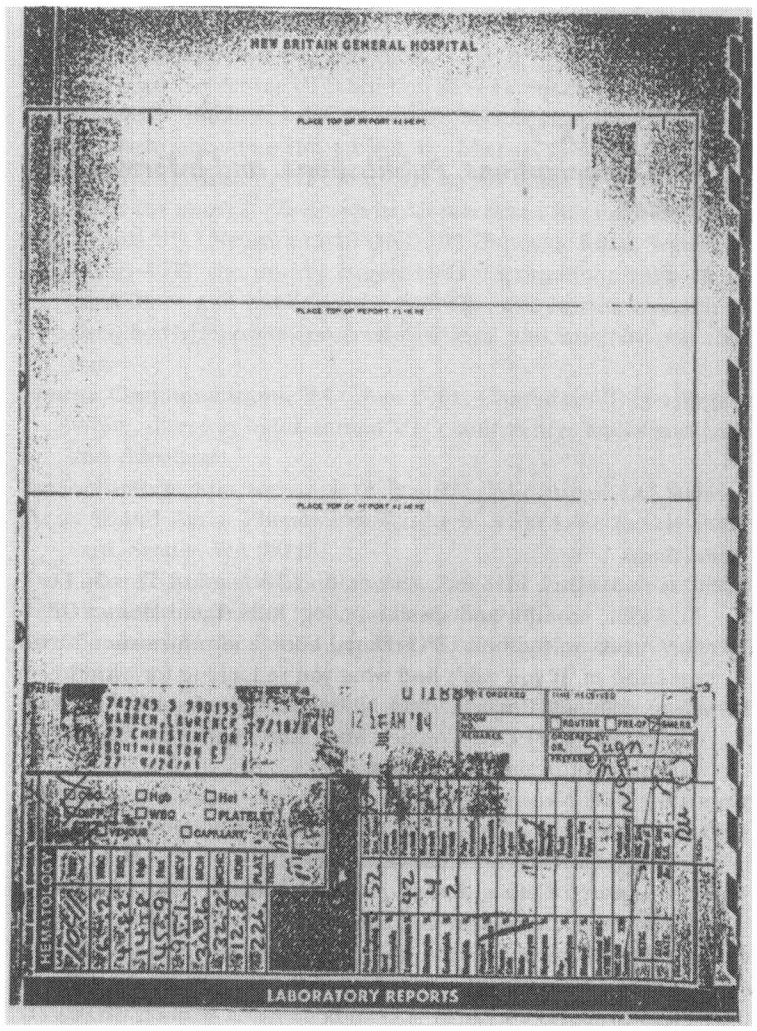

So, what street drug is it that causes the body's white blood cells to show signs of having been heavily dosed by radiation, one symptom of which is occasionally hemorrhaging through the skin? And to a degree that the attending doctors would have expected to see after twenty years, not four years.

Regarding a second anomalous injury Warren suffered, setting the scene first:

> "The red light cleared the pines bordering the field and quickly made a downward arc until it was directly over the illuminated fog. Only about twenty feet above the ground, the object was now stationary and roughly the size of a basketball. I had never seen its color before, but red comes closest.
>
> As my mind tried to register what I was looking at, the ball of light exploded in a blinding flash. Shards of light and particles fell onto the fog. Several cops ran into the woods. I couldn't move; I tried to cover my eyes, but was too late. I was numb and very likely in shock. Why I didn't run, I don't know. I wanted to, but I was cemented in place.
>
> The explosion produced no noticeable heat. But now, right in front of me, was a machine occupying the spot where the fog had been." (*LAEG*, page 45)

The symptoms of what would soon be diagnosed as a serious eye problem manifested themselves almost immediately:

> "We got back to Central Security Control at about 4:30 A.M. I returned my weapon to the armory, then joined other groups from my flight in the lounge to drink coffee and stare at the walls. At 6:30, A-Flight reported for the day shift. Some of the men began making jokes about little green men and flying saucers. We were too drained to react to them; we only shook our heads in disgust. I was relieved from duty, caught a police bus, then went straight to my room and collapsed on the floor.
>
> My eyes hurt. I had a bad taste in my mouth and a ringing in my ears." (*LAEG*, page 48)

Larry made an appointment to visit the base health clinic as his eye problems grew worse:

Chapter 6: Anomalous Injuries

"My eye sight had been impaired since that explosion of light just before the UFO had appeared. Sunlight hurt my eyes; what appeared to be sea horses floated in my line of sight. I had gone to the clinic on Bentwaters for an exam; a doctor told me I might have burns to my retinas. He sent me to RAF Lakenheath for a more in-depth eye exam in early February. It was later confirmed that I had been exposed to a source of high intensity light that had caused a degree of damage to my sight. The ranking doctor explained it was as if I had looked directly at a welder's torch for twenty minutes without blinking. He noted the beginnings of scar tissue forming at the inner corner of each eye, recommending a powerful antibiotic eye drop prescription, and possibly glasses. I tried to tell the doctor what had happened, but he didn't want to know." (*LAEG*, page 71)

What is the evidence backing up this injury to his eyes?

USAF form 490, the medical appointment card noting his 2 February 1981 visit to the RAF Lakenheath Eye and Ear Clinic.

A close-up of the form set off by the dot shows the attending physician's diagnosis of the problem:

69

Halt in Woodbridge

Close up of Larry Warren's medical form.

It reads "OPTI/Ret Burn EXP – optical retinal burn exposure, certainly something that would have been picked up during his Air Force induction physical had he entered the service with this condition.

In what possible manner could such an injury be the result of 'drugs' or alleged drug addiction any more than the previous injury? The fact is, it couldn't, despite what Charles Halt wants to believe, imagine, or accuse Larry Warren of.

I can think of no situation where it would be appropriate for a military officer to mock injuries sustained by an enlisted person as a direct result of their having followed the orders they had been given. That, in effect, is what Charles Halt did in ignoring and demeaning the seriousness of Warren's injuries. But another officer reacted far differently when he learned of the nature of Warren's injuries. Peter Hill-Norton was a retired British Navy admiral and a former Ministry of Defence Chief of Staff. Following his retirement from the MoD Admiral Lord Peter became a Member of Parliament (MP). On 28 October 1997 he asked this question of Lord Gilbert, the then-Secretary for Defence:

> Hill-Norton: "What information they have on the medical problems experienced by various United States Air Force personnel based at RAF Bentwaters and RAF Woodbridge, which stemmed from their being involved in the so-called Rendlesham Forest incident, in December 1980."
>
> Lord Gilbert: "Information on medical matters relating to US personnel is a matter for the US Air Force." (*LAEG,* page xxxiii)

This was far from the only thing that had made Lord Hill-Norton such a staunch supporter of Larry Warren's, more on which is covered later.

> (Ben Emlyn-Jones in voiceover) At about 25:07 I can hear Halt talking in background. He says something like 'Well, Peter Robbins pestered just about everyone on the planet trying to find...'

This on a personal note—I was mortified to learn from Charles via Ben that I "pestered just about everyone on the planet" during the course of writing *Left At East Gate* with Larry. If you were among those I pestered, I hope you will accept my sincerest apologies for having done so. I don't know what happened to my manners during those nine years of investigation and research. I do however appreciate the colonel's acknowledging that I am "not a dumb guy."

> (Ben in voiceover) Round about 26:25 Halt in background: **I feel sorry for Larry Warren. I think he's a basket case.**
>
> HALT (on being asked about medical treatment and the VA, at 28:00):
>
> **And I think they should treat Larry Warren too. I mean, despite the fact he probably needs some other kind of counselling or help** (laughs and general sniggering from several people).
>
> BRENDA BUTLER: That's where he (Larry) (inaudible) put the UFO (inaudible) radiation the night (inaudible).
>
> **Well, he's been smoking them funny cigarettes again.**

Let me remind the colonel of something he already knows. Prior to any shift change in guard duty there is an obligatory procedure known as 'Guard Mount.' In it, personnel who will be going on duty are fully vetted to learn if, for example, they had a beer with lunch, taken an over-the-counter cold tablet, or ingested *anything* that might impair their judgement, vision, reflexes or powers of observation. Lives have been lost for less and *any* violation of this Air Force statute is punishable under the Uniform Code of Military Justice (UCMJ). To suggest that someone who had passed this this procedure, then been posted to guard duty, and then lit up a joint, is the same as accusing them of endangering the safety and welfare of other personnel so assigned, and endangering the safety and security of the entire base should a worst case scenario arise. The colonel is correct in observing that there were drug busts on base. But in this instance to jokingly suggest that the cause of Security Specialist Warren's believing he was involved in a UFO incident was that he had smoked marijuana while on duty is beyond insulting. The only other person I'm aware of who ever made the same suggestion was UFO debunker Philip Klass and in some ways he and the colonel have a lot in common.

Did Ben Emlyn-Jones violate Charles Halt's and David Bryant's 'right of privacy' by filming part of their (and others) walk in the forest? No. It was being filmed as per his agreement with John Hanson. Did Ben Emlyn-Jones in effect violate that agreement after turning off his camera, then going on to make notes characterizing some of the remarks made and exchanged?' Perhaps. But given the insights yielded by his having done so? Do I care? Not really.

Chapter 7:

The Underground

Returning to the presentation in the Woodbridge Community Building:

CH: "His security clearance was upgraded. We in the base did not upgrade security clearances. That would require a lot of action, a lot of investigation. You don't upgrade security clearance just like that."

No page number is given for this charge, but the reference to a security clearance upgrade appears on page 53. Yet again Mr. Halt presents something he alleges Larry having said that proves to be completely untrue. What is he referring to here? The debriefing that Warren and other witnesses were ordered to attend the day after the third night's events. It was conducted by a Commander Richardson of the Office of Naval Intelligence (ONI) and two men in suits representing the Armed Forces Security Service (AFSS), a field arm of the National Security Agency. During the debriefing "We were told that our security clearances had been upgraded (I had had a secret clearance at the time). In the event we talked about the UFO we'd face stiffer penalties for doing so." (*LAEG*, page 53)

Halt correctly states that "we in the base did not upgrade security clearances," this while fully knowing from his reading of *Left At East Gate* that none of the three debriefers were in any way associated with the base nor were any of them Air Force personnel. And who said that "his security clearance was upgraded"? Certainly not Larry Warren. What he and the others were *told* by Commander Richardson was that their clearances had been upgraded. In fact Warren's remained the same and I expect those of the other assembled personnel did as well.

Underground facility. Let's talk about that! I was taken to the photo lab, and put in an elevator and my ears crackled or whatever as I went down in this facility that had a UFO in it. The medical staff that examined me, they had a cafeteria. The picture he identified and has pictures in his book is a command post. The command post is a hardened facility, reinforced concrete, it's on 3 feet of reinforced concrete, has black shields around it, has doors like a bank vault. Big steels that slide. One way in, one way out. Now there is an emergency escape hatch that is sealed, and we never open that seal, but that was for an emergency. It could not have been the command post. We don't have any underground facilities at Bentwaters. Now in the 90s they built a new squadron building on the far side of the field, and it may have an underground facility, but that was in the 90s, and that was nothing like described as this facility.

No page number given but a full account of these events can be found on pages 58 through 63. Reviewing this new batch of alleged charges:

I was taken to the photo lab.

Larry Warren never said, alleged or written that he was taken to the base photo lab. Not in *Left At East Gate* nor anywhere else. The reason being, he wasn't.

(I was) put in an elevator and my ears crackled or whatever

This is what Larry wrote about the above:

"Suddenly I felt fresh air hit my face, I could smell it. I was now out of the car and walking or moving in some direction. I sensed people around me, but I was never touched or pushed. The next thing was a definite sensation of descent, as if I were in an elevator, causing

Chapter 7: The Underground

pressure changes in my ears. Then I lost consciousness." (*LAEG*, page 60)

The very real sense that he was descending in an elevator was fully captured during his July 1995 hypnotic regression with Budd Hopkins:

LW. I can see the back corner of an elevator, a small room, and, and it's very rapid; it's, there's descent... I see people standing [inaudible]. I'm facing, I'm facing down.

BH. Um hum. Now let's see the positions you would feel the parts of your body, what is pinching where you're being held.

LW. [exhales] The uh, ribcage, pelvis, and my ankles, and prob... uh, my forehead, but there's something uh... the sides of my head... it's uh, near the top.

BH. So this is rapid descent; still, is there any conversation you pick up, from the people you're with?

LW. I hear, a conversation, I can't uh, it's all like a record, a slow record. There's a [pause], a, that fades... that's... that's not becoming clear, anymore. [pause] That room is not clear anymore.

BH. [inaudible] about the room?

LW. This uh, this elevator is not clear, it's a – its, the imagery, not there... it's not a..[pause] at all.

BH. Um hum. Do you feel at all you've been hit again by this stuff, or do you...

LW. No. I feel a void.

BH. Um hum. Okay, so when, do you feel the elevator stopped some point? You said you felt a descent.

LW. ... I just feel, going down, like the Empire State Building. Uh, that was, that was it.

BH. [pause] Now what's the next thing, that becomes clear, next change; all this is very chronological. Is this elevator feeling, the rapid descent, that your nose is running and so forth... let's see, what happens next that's, a memorable kind of change. (*LAEG*, pages 383-384)

I went down in this facility that had a UFO in it.

Warren's best memory was of being taken down into what he sensed, felt, deduced, was a large facility below the base – or that he was certainly made to feel and believe this to be the case. Regarding the UFO:

> "I stepped into the confined area and felt as if I was no longer on earth. I found myself looking into a *gigantic* dark cavernous space. It reminded me of the interior of the Houston Astrodome in a strange way. Beads of humidity rolled down the other side of the seamless glass. Far below, I saw movement on a liquid black floor -- perhaps people, perhaps not. Also, an object much like the one I'd seen the night before, but not so illuminated, was resting in a far corner of the facility. In the black void were other strange objects, all different in shape, slowly flying across my line of sight." (*LAEG*, page 60)

The medical staff that examined me.

Warren clearly recalls the following, also while in regression with Hopkins:

> B.H. ...let's see, what happens next that's, a memorable kind of change.
>
> LW. [pause] I'm sitting upright, and there's a, [pause] doctor...
>
> BH. Um hum.
>
> LW. ...eyewash? You know, eyewash -- Visine, a, and a cup, and a -- my eyes, burn. And my -- he wipes my face off, with a cloth. And uh, sitting in a chair.
>
> BH. Um hum. Can you, now that you see a little better, could you see anything about, this doctor? Does he have a laminated name tag or anything like that?
>
> LW. No. Uh, receding hairline, dark, short, military, haircut. Ah... six foot, and um, it's hard to say, brown eyes, nose kind of like mine, and um, thirty-nine, forty.

Chapter 7: The Underground

BH. Um hum. What does he say to you?

LW. Nothing. Nothing at all... nothing...

BH. And is this doctor someone you may have seen before somewhere on the base, or is he some...

LW. No. No, but my impression is, of a doctor. The white coat, and the room is, very medically oriented (pause), like an emergency room. There are some other areas with curtains, and there's a door to this room and glass windows with, in the door and in the office, the room, and you can see other areas like an emergency room.

BH. Um hum.

LW. [long pause] I have no clue what a... really, no clue, at all, with... uh...

BH. Were you able to speak? Ask?

LW. I, I'm just not asking; I'm just sitting, and looking [slight laugh]... I've been in a clinic on Bentwaters -this isn't it. We only have one, on the base, it's not it.

BH. Um hum. (*LAEG*, page 384)

They had a cafeteria.

Apparently they did, or at least an area that served as one. The first thing Larry remembers when he comes to following his descent in what seemed to have been an elevator is this:

> "A hamburger was on a tray in front of me, but I cannot remember eating at all. The lighting was strange, the walls were covered in cream-colored tiles. Next I was walking along a hallway." (*LAEG*, page 60) That's what he remembers. Or was made to remember.

An important though often sensationalized aspect of Larry Warren's account is the existence of an underground facility located below RAF Bentwaters and perhaps the twin base complex itself. Given the controversial and often-attacked nature of this claim, I continued to work any avenues of investigation

77

open to me even after our book was first published. Two breaks came in quick succession toward the end of June 1997:

"The first was on June 27 when a local Suffolk investigator introduced me to "B," an independent civilian contractor who had been employed by the Air Force for more than twenty years, and who still held all the appropriate base security clearances. B and the crews he supervised had worked all over the Bentwaters complex, and occasionally under it. I interviewed him as we sat in a van parked by the back gate of the now-decommissioned RAF Bentwaters, this while Larry and three of our friends were inside the base reconnoitering and watching out for security patrol vehicles.

B told me that underground concrete tunnels ringed the base just below the surface. He had been down in them a number of times and thought they connected to the underground bunkers. RAF Bentwaters possessed the largest bomb dump in all of Europe he said, and huge banks of infrared lights as wide as a car were used to maintain the ordinance at a certain temperature – one hundred and three degrees Fahrenheit. All of the fixtures were still in place down there, as were the huge generators which powered them. B went on to say that on the far side of the concrete bomb-proof hangar visible from our vehicle was a mound where that concrete tunnel finishes, bricked up with concrete bricks. At the far side of the mound is what B felt were false water tanks. It was made to look authentic, he suspected that the tanks were made to lift out, below which was a staircase to the underground bunker.

Following "B's" instructions, our team behind the wire - Larry accompanied by several colleagues, radioed in via walkie talkie. Apparently the first manhole cover they'd found into the 'water pipe' had been welded shut. This made no sense to B. The manhole covers go completely round the base, literally, and B had been down most of them. But all for water? B didn't think so: "You're kidding. That [indicating] goes to a reservoir that's never been used. [In the tunnels] there's perfect air. There's not an air problem. We took an air thing [air quality measuring device] down, you know, we done an air test: perfect air. It don't makes sense mate. They were put in there for water so why bother?

Two days later a close friend in the area introduced me to George

Chapter 7: The Underground

Nursey, a resident of nearby Woodbridge. Between 1988 and 1990 George had been employed as a quantity surveyor by the Property Services Agency (PSA), a now-defunct British governmental organization which looked after the upkeep of military and other official buildings. One afternoon he found himself alone in the PSA office and on an impulse, pulled a set of architect's plans out of an unsecured drawer, plans which clearly indicated three tunnels running between Woodbridge and Bentwaters. George estimated from the scale that they could have easily accommodated the combined population of both bases at the time, that being about four and a half thousand people. He described the tunnels as about the same size as the Channel Tunnels that connect Dover and Calais. He also stated that there is an area near the Bentwaters perimeter where "there's a part of ground that *dips* [all emphasis his]. Now that *looks* like its subsidence from a tunnel that has been bored, years ago. You know where I'm talking about, and if you look, down a line, you can see a dip, and that's a man-made dip. It's as simple as that. And it goes into the base that way, through the fence, you can *see it*, and that is interesting to me." (*LAEG*, pages xxx-xxxii)

I believe Charles Halt is wrong and that a very real 'someplace' does exist below this Suffolk airbase or airbases. Secured underground facilities should never be dismissed as fantasies of the conspiracy-minded, sci-fi fans or other 'believer' types. They are very much a reality and exist all over the world. Responsible authors, researchers and investigators have named and identified, verified and confirmed their presence for decades. Their purposes are as diverse as they are numerous, be they governmental, private sector or intelligence purposed. They are used for medical research and containment, data storage, military industrial usage, emergency planning and occupation and research and development. They are as real as any above ground factory, business office or shopping center. Do some homework and find out for yourself.

With respect to Charles Halt and the underground, what can we deduce? One of three things. That it does not exist and he is telling us the truth. That it does exist and he is not telling us the truth. Or that it does exist and he is not aware of it. A thought I had was, when it comes to military staffing at a base such as Bentwaters, those serving in important but temporary command positions simply may not be cleared to know anything about this other facility. It's nothing personal. It's called *need to know*. Many years ago, this former deputy base commander learned that he did not 'need to know' why the National Security Agency has maintained an interest in Larry Warren, John Burroughs, and certain other Rendlesham witnesses since just after the RFI. Then, as pointed out to me by a former Air Force officer, Halt, as Deputy Base Commander, would have at least known that these facilities existed. Base facilities, their functions, and maintenance are things base commanders and their deputies have as prime responsibilities. We will likely never know the answer to this question.

Another thing you need to know. With the rarest of exceptions, the records of every single individual who ever served in the United States military since the War for Independence are housed at the massive National Military Records Repository in St. Louis Missouri. I've done research there and the place is massive.

That's where Charles Halt's military records are kept, among millions of others. But it's not where you'll find the records of Warren, Burroughs, and other RFI witnesses. They are housed in Ft. Meade Maryland, home of the National Security Agency.[6]

The picture he identified and has pictures in his book is a command post. … and that was nothing like described as this facility.

Larry has never identified the structure that appears in the

---

[6] One source of information on underground bases, facilities and tunnels are the books of Dr. Richard Sauder. *Underwater and Underground Bases* was published by Adventures Unlimited Press in 2001 and *Hidden In Plain Sight* by Keyhole Publishing Co. in 2010. Sauder is also the author of *Underground Bases and Tunnels*.

Chapter 7: The Underground

photo section of our book – to me or to anyone else – as *anything* other than what it is: a conventional command post made of reinforced concrete. And there are no "pictures" of it in *Left At East Gate,* only a single photograph. So what's this allegation all about?

When the manuscript for *Left At East Gate* was being finalized by our publisher at their Lower Manhattan office, I was living in Midtown Manhattan and Larry in Vermont, so it logically fell to me and not Larry to irregularly return to the officers of Marlowe & Company to complete work on a number of minor loose ends before the book was ready for its press run. One of these the tasks was to supply captions for the few photos we had neglected to caption when I handed in the completed floppy discs in May of that year. The photo Charles refers to is indeed a command post and in the terms he describes it. The wording I chose for the caption was "Earthen bunker concealing an unspecified underground facility at RAF Bentwaters. (note blowers for ventilation)," and Charles is absolutely correct in pointing out that my choice of words may have been misleading to some readers.

This picture is very similar to the one that appears in Left At East Gate. Photo: Peter Robbins.

My intention in wording the caption the way I did was to make the point that *somewhere* below this completely conventional

81

command post lay a deeper secured facility. I would certainly word it differently if I were to do so today – but let it be absolutely understood that my co-author was in no way responsible for the wording of this caption or ever mischaracterized the nature or purpose of the structure in the photograph.

"I was kidnapped, and bundled into a car. A limousine. A Cadillac. An Imperial. I was gassed and I was taken to this facility." Nonsense. It had New York plates. He remembers in hypnosis. Well why didn't someone check those plates out in 1983 if they're gonna write a book then. It would be very easy to verify the plates at that time. Didn't happen. Or maybe it did and there were no such plates.

Taking the above in two parts:

"I was kidnapped, and bundled into a car. A limousine. A Cadillac. An Imperial. I was gassed and I was taken to this facility." Nonsense.

What Halt dismisses as "nonsense" was anything but to Larry Warren, Adrian Bustinza, and the other men who were subjected to unspecified procedures and 'debriefing' techniques. I'm going to make an educated guess that for them it was a frightening, disorienting, and entirely life-changing experience, and in no way for the better. However or wherever these events transpired, they live with the PTSD after effects and that is not "nonsense" either. This is how Warren consciously remembered what happened:

> ...The dorm phone rang, and my friend, Dave, got up and answered it. I heard him say from the hall, "Yes, he's right here," as he pointed the receiver in my direction. I had a sinking feeling as I approached the phone. Let's face it, every time the phone rang that

Chapter 7: The Underground

day, I found myself in more hot water!

"Hello, Airman Warren?" "Yes, this is Warren." I didn't know the male voice on the other end. The call sounded as if it were a long distance connection, as if the caller's voice were in a vacuum. "Airman Warren, could you meet a car in the dorm parking lot in twenty minutes?" I asked, "Who are you?" The voice responded that wasn't important, "Please meet the car in *twenty* minutes." I asked how I would recognize the car. The voice said, "It will be a dark blue sedan, upscale, you'll know it when you see it!" I asked if his request concerned the UFO incident. "Yes," the voice responded. "Am I in trouble? Will I be late for my shift? I have to work tonight."

The answer to both questions was "no." He continued: "You do not have to be in uniform, and Warren, remember, twenty minutes. Okay? Another airman will be with you. You won't miss the car, will you?" "No Sir." The man hung up his phone. While staring at some pro-IRA graffiti on the wall in front of my face, I hesitantly did the same.

Upstairs in my room, I grabbed a heavy jacket and headed for the parking lot. The weather had turned colder and more winter-like, but the brisk air sharpened my senses. I wished I had been stationed in California or a warmer climate. Anywhere but England; it just wasn't fun anymore.

I could see the car now; it looked like a Lincoln town car. As I got closer, its orange and blue New York State plates made me strangely homesick. Across the lot, another airman walked toward the car. It was Adrian Bustinza. He had been in the field with me the night before.

As we neared the car, I turned to Adrian and said, "How are you doing?" He just waved back. The car was in the far end of the lot near the new housing construction site. Not a soul was in the lot with us. The driver and passenger side doors opened. Two men got out of the car; they were dressed in civilian clothes. I can't remember their faces. They opened the doors to the backseat. Once I was next to the car, I looked at the interior before I climbed in. I knew something was wrong: the interior was just too bright, with a greenish glow, as if the dash lights were amplified five hundred times. It was eerie. The men said nothing, and as I bent forward to get in, everything went black. I was in a void. I knew I was seated in the car, and I knew Adrian was next to me, but I couldn't talk or move. However, I could hear. I felt like I'd been anesthetized. I heard no conversation in the car, though I wanted to, to hear *anything* to take me out of my semi-conscious state.

But that's all I can remember until I heard the engine of an A-10 taking off. I was on the Bentwater flight line. I knew it, but that was all I knew. Suddenly I felt fresh air hit my face, I could smell it. I was now out of the car and walking or moving in some direction. I sensed people around me, but I was never touched or pushed.(and then) The next thing was a definite sensation of descent, as if I were in an elevator, causing pressure changes in my ears. Then I lost consciousness." (*LAEG,* pages 58-69)

He remembers in hypnosis.

He did remember certain things under hypnosis. I know. I sat a few feet from him as a witness. Anyone familiar with the practice of *responsible,* carefully administered regressive hypnosis knows that the details which sometimes emerge while the individual is under may differ from what they had always recalled in their conscious lives. This is especially true when the underlying memories being explored have been blocked, or locked away due to trauma, shock or other unpleasant reasons. This, not surprisingly, was the case when Larry Warren.

For the first eight years I worked with my co-author (our book took nine years to complete) he never showed any interest in undergoing regressive hypnosis in order to return to the night following the UFO incident. His general response was he remembered what he remembered and that was good enough for him, at least until the summer of 1995. What changed was Larry's willingness to face whatever might await him in returning to that night. His regression with Budd Hopkins took place 15 July 1995.

Chapter 7: The Underground

Budd Hopkins was one of the most respected people in the history of UFO studies. He was *the* pioneer investigator of the scientific study of the UFO abduction phenomenon, and a brilliant, self-trained investigative writer. Budd was the founder of a nonprofit named the Intruders Foundation (IF). It was dedicated to the study of the abduction phenomenon and established to offer public education regarding this highly misunderstood subject as well as provide assistance and support for those who had actually experienced it.

The colonel's sarcastic "limousine, Cadillac, Imperial" remark aside, the car that had "looked like a Lincoln town car" was of similar appearance but not a Lincoln after all:

BH. What do you see when you go outside?

LW. Ah, streetlights are just going on, car pulling up near the stairway, staff sergeant [pause] who goes in the building, downstairs. I, I'm looking in the parking lot. I'm looking at the parking lot. New housing. Over the fence, there's a car, there...

BH. And you said...

LW. ...near a dumpster.

BH. You said there's a black car that you're supposed to meet. Is that the one you see over there?

LW. Yeah.

BH. Um hum. By the dumpster?

LW. Right.

BH. Let's get a look at that car.

LW. [Pause] A black... silver -- chrome trim, whitewalls, spoked hubcaps...

BH: What kind of car is it you think?

LW. I think an '80 Caddy.

BH. Um hum.

Well why didn't someone check those plates out in 1983 if

they're gonna write a book then. It would be very easy to verify the plates at that time. Didn't happen. Or maybe it did and there were no such plates.

Budd did in fact recover two slight variations on the plate number:

BH. Did they identify themselves by name and rank or anything?

LW. No but they're asking *me* if I am who I am. Bustinza's in his uh, working greens, so he's dressed. I'm feeling self-conscious, um, "Yes, I am," and uh... [change in pitch and tone; now speaking slightly higher and faster] One of them has gone around the front of the car to the other side and he is opening the... front door, and... kinda looking at us basically. The back door of my side, on the left side, and uh, the New York plate, I see, I can see the plate very clearly, I'm right on the corner.

BH. Can you read it?

LW. It is a New York State, '81 is the..

BH. Is the year?

LW. No, '81 is the tag, the registration tag on the back. There is uh, God: 6J9-2B. New York, and '81 is there, February '81 is their expiration. [two or three words to self, inaudible]

BH. Want to give me that again so I make sure I got it?

LW. 2J1... 6B, its... 2J1-6B, there's someth... [pause] January '81. '81 January is how its...

BH. Yeah, okay. Do you look at that for any particular reason, or just casually notice that?

LW. Because it's New York.

BH. I see. Okay

The reason no one checked those plates in 1983 was because the "someone" was not writing a book in 1983, and because he was still twelve years away from his hypnotic regression with Hopkins.

It would be very easy to verify the plates at that time.

Yes, I expect it would have been.

Didn't happen. Or maybe it did and there were no such plates.

Yes, it did happen, and whether or not the plates ever prove to be traceable or not, the colonel not only knew the numbers on them from reading his copy of *Left At East Gate,* he also knew them because he got to listen to his *very own* audiocassette copy of Larry's regression with Budd. How, and why he managed this is something we'll come to later.

Chapter 8:

The Colonel vs. *Left At East Gate,* Part II

Page 136, All the squadrons on the base had a big meeting to discuss it. Nonsense. We didn't have any big meeting on the base.

Would any member of Charles Halt's audience have understood what was supposed to be the source of the claim above? The only answer is Larry Warren. But *did* Larry Warren actually say or allege this? The answer to that would be no. How can I be sure? Because the colonel is making reference to a remark made by another SP, that being Greg Battram, and this during the course of his 7 February 1984 interview with Larry Fawcett.

Security Police Specialists Warren and Battram at Awards Night honoring the 81st SPS 1981 unit citation, best in USAFE (United States Air Force in Europe).

Greg, also attached to the 81st Security Police, was another of the D Flight SPs who were witness to a part of the third night's encounter in Capel Green. He and another cop had been on patrol that night and were driving around the RAF Woodbridge perimeter road when they sighted the lights and drove toward them. They arrived in the area on their own and not as part of the contingent that had departed the Main Gate of RAF Bentwaters together. I transcribed the audiotaped interview myself for inclusion in *Left At East Gate*. It was one of a number of cassettes of interviews conducted with involved Air Force personnel that Larry Fawcett had given Larry Warren. This is the relevant part of that interview:

LF. Was there a lot of commotion about this in the next couple of days after that?

GB. Not really officially I think. Not that you could really see. We got talked to the next day and [they] said "be quiet."

LF. Because Larry, Bustinza was telling me they were called down to the communications shack and all were debriefed on what they had seen and so forth.

GB. Yes, because we had a meeting, the Planning and Program Section did. Every commander of every squadron or tenant organization section was there. It was like the base security council met. Then there were some other people that I had never seen before, and they turned out to be from Washington.

LF. From where?

GB. From Washington apparently.

LF. And they debriefed you?

GB. Yes, they gave their little speech, it was all discussed at the meeting. Get the word out to everyone, don't spread any rumors and that kind of stuff. And calm it down and talk it down.

The colonel might argue that my including this part of Greg's transcript communicated something that was false to the best of his knowledge. Or that he wanted the audience to think was false. I had simply transcribed the words of the interviewer and interviewee as accurately as I always did for inclusion in our book. Charles Halt knew exactly what he was doing in choosing not to identify the party in question. The question here is isn't, did this meeting take place, though I would tend to take Greg's word over Halt's at this point. The question is that the speaker again misled his audience to believe it was Larry Warren rather than Greg Battram who had made this statement, thus showing Warren to be wrong again.

Claims he had a side arm. We do not give Security Police side arms.

Once again, the Woodbridge audience could only assume that Halt was referring to Larry Warren here. In truth, he was talking about Adrian Bustinza. This is how this little slight-of-hand was accomplished, via an excerpt from Larry Fawcett's 1984 interview with Adrian:

LF. Okay. From there you took a right and went up into the wooded area.

AB. Correct.

LF. He says when you got to like a sort of staging point up in there, there were other vehicles there when you got there.

AB. Right.

LF. Okay. You got out of the vehicles. They took the weapons away from you.

AB. Well, they didn't take mine.

LF. They didn't take yours?

AB. No sir.

LF. Okay. Well...

AB. They, well, let me see -- no, mine was taken away but I had a side arm also.

LF. You had a side arm?

AB. They did take our big weapons away which were M-16's.

What we have is one more decision on Charles Halt's part to intentionally mislead the people attending his talk with a worthless, misrepresented allegation solely geared to make Larry Warren look bad. And while Security Police were not issued side arms, there was a good reason for Adrian Bustinza's having been issued one that night, and the deputy base commander should have been aware of it.

Major Zickler was there and fell in the mud. Major Zickler was at the party.

I will gladly take Mr. Halt's word that Major Malcolm Zickler also attended the same party he did—for part of the evening at least. But according to Charles, once Lt. Englund approached him there and told him, "They're back," the then-lieutenant colonel left the festivities, returned to his residence, changed into appropriate field gear, assembled the team we hear in the recording he made in the forest that night, and never returned to the party. Our speaker would have had no way of accounting for the whereabouts of his fellow officer from the moment he left the party until the two next saw each other, whenever that was.

Would the colonel have us believe that the major, who also happened to Chief of the Security Police, had remained uninformed of this most recent UFO incident and instead pleasantly wiled away the remainder of the evening at a social event at the same time as a large contingent of *his men* were being deployed in the Rendlesham Forest to investigate and otherwise take part in an extremely important incident fraught with potentially grave consequences for the security of the entire Twin Base Complex? If anything, the major would have been informed in as timely a manner as Halt was, and being a real leader from what I've learned about him, joined his men at the staging area as soon as possible, which in fact is just what happened. Larry Warren:

"We continued slowly down the narrow dirt logging road. After

Halt in Woodbridge

approximately one-half mile, the trucks and cars entered a large clearing. Other trucks were already parked in the area; we stopped. I got off the pickup and waited for orders. I saw that about fifteen men in uniform and several others in civilian clothes were heading down a narrow trail on foot. I watched as their flashlights faded into the darkness.

Just then, the Chief of Security Police arrived at the site, and stepped from his car into a rather large mud puddle. We broke up over his mishap. It was the last time I would laugh that night." (*LAEG*, page 43)

Adrian Bustinza's actual recollection negates Halt's belief as well. From Adrian's April 1984 interview with Larry Fawcett:

LF. Okay. As you were going through now, Larry said all of a sudden, they could see lights coming through the woods and he could also hear helicopters over above.

AB. Yes, a squadron, pararescue squadron was activated.

LF. Pararescue. Where were they from? Woodbridge?

AB. Woodbridge. they weren't very far away as a matter of fact.

LF. Do you know how many were up at the time?

AB. I recall Major Zickler said scramble two, I believe he said.

LF. Two?

AB. Two. I think that's what he prescribed, two.

I think the only reason Col Halt wanted his audience to believe that Maj. Zickler stayed on at the party after Charles had departed was that it was one more thing to make Larry appear mistaken or confused about.

Chapter 9:

"They Talk About Cloud Busters"

They talk about Cloud Busters. This is a good one. You're gonna get a kick out of this part. We had cloudbusters, what do you call them? They call them, the guys who made and designed them. They actually probably do work to alter the weather, and he saw these devices on Bentwaters base... My next door neighbor was Karl. Karl had a great sense of humor and was quite a character. We were pretty good friends. We knew when the Russian satellites flew over. We discussed it all the time. We knew when they were going over. There was only two of them in those days. So Karl made a bunch of dummy missiles and dummy odds and ends and we'd paint them different colors and we'd move them around the base every time the satellite would go over, and that's what pictured as the cloud busters. Even Georgina Bruni has it in her book. You'll see... called a cloud buster. It is not a cloud buster. It was a dummy designed to drive folks crazy trying to figure out what we were doing. Pictures in (inaudible) and book.

First thing, I was impressed to learn that Mr. Halt seems to take the proven weather-modification abilities of the Reich 'cloudbuster' seriously. His point though is Larry Warren mistakenly confused one of Karl's dummy missiles for an actual cloudbuster. It's fair to assume that Karl's dummy missiles were long cylinder-shaped objects that tapered to points. An actual cloudbuster apparatus as designed by Dr. Wilhelm Reich in the early Nineteen Fifties, would have been easy to distinguish from one of Karl's constructions. They consist of a series long fixed pipes, usually with one row above and one below, that are each connected to hollow lengths of industrial BX cable. The ends of these cables are submerged in a body of water or well with the

Halt in Woodbridge

water acting as natural attractor. This in turn stimulates directional movement in the atmosphere.

This cloudbuster was built and successfully operated by Dr. James DeMeo, Director of the Orgone Biophysical Research Labortory (also known as 'Greensprings Laboratory) located near Ashland Oregon. Photo: Peter Robbins.

Had Larry Warren been the only witness to identify a cloudbuster near the RAF Bentwaters flight line I would not have included it on my chapter covering this period. Not because I didn't believe him, but because the account of his involvement in the RFI was challenging enough to present to readers in an objective, grounded manner without bringing in the controversial discoveries of the late Dr. Wilhelm Reich. It's a shame for the audience that the colonel fails to inform them that Warren's testimony was fully confirmed by two other unsolicited and highly credible Air Force witnesses. Forgetfulness? Perhaps. Perhaps not.

Larry and I met Howard and Grace on August 25, 1991 in Glens Falls, New York. They'd found his number in the phone book and had called to say how disappointed they were to have missed a talk we'd given on the RFI the day before. We invited them over to Larry's apartment for coffee and conversation and ended up recording an interview with them in the process. The married couple were both honorably retired USAF sergeants who had served together at the Twin Base Complex in 1982 and

Chapter 9: "They Talk About Cloud Busters"

A cloudbuster operated by Dr. Richard Blasband. Photo credit: the American College of Orgonomy, Princeton, NJ.

1983. They had no problem whatsoever identifying a slide photo of a Reich cloudbuster as almost identical (except considerably smaller) than the one they remembered near the Bentwaters flight line. And their account was hardly hidden away in some arcane source. Charles would have had to have read it on pages 51 and 52 of his copy of *Left At East Gate.* Because this easily available first-rate evidence was intentionally withheld by Charles Halt, his audience was yet again left to wonder about the veracity of Larry Warren's account. I do not believe there is any way that this could have been accidental.

"Even Georgina Bruni has it in her book. You'll see… called a cloud buster. It is not a cloud buster. It was a dummy…"

Yes, even Georgina has it in her book, though it turns out that the 'it' referred to is not the 'it' the colonel hopes you will believe it is. Then again, throughout the final half hour of his talk he seems confident enough that no one will take the time to confirm any of his accusations against Larry, *Left At East Gate,*

Halt in Woodbridge

Georgina Bruni. Photo circa 2000. Photographer unknown.

or me for themselves.

Georgina Bruni was a smart, savvy woman and a member in good standing of the London social scene for many years. She was, among other things, a private investigator, founder of one of the internet's first on-line magazines, a decidedly upscale gossip columnist, researcher into the unexplained who maintained friendships with UK movers and shakers including members of Parliament, the Ministry of Defence, and members of the Royal family's various staffs. Between 1998 and 2001 she

96

was a Special Correspondent for my website, Ufocity.com (1998-2004).

Charles's reference to her is in regard to the book she authored on the Rendlesham Forest incident titled *You Can't Tell the People*. Larry and I were introduced to her in 1997 by Nick Pope, then an official with the Ministry of Defence. Georgina and I remained friends until her untimely death in 2008. After reading the inscribed copy of *LAEG* that Larry and I gave her in the summer of 1997 she became so interested in the RFI that she decided to write her own book about it. Georgina already had an interest in 'weather weapons' and *Left At East Gate* led her to develop an interest in Reich cloudbuster technology as well. At her request I sent her an assortment of articles on the subject as well as two related papers of my own. This email from her underscores this fact:

Date: Tue, 17 Nov 1998 13:05:03 +0000

To: Peter Robbins <probbins@teamcpm.com>

From: georgina@easynet.co.uk

Subject: Re: Dearest Peter

Peter. Just a quickie. I'm interested in your weather weapon theory. Did you know that one of the first radar scientists from Bawdsey/Orfordness went on to work with weapon weapons. He ended up making rain in Australia. His name - Edward Bowen. worked just down the road from Woodbridge. Hugs, Georgina.

She was already hard at work on her investigation when she sent this email. While she and Larry tangled on a number of issues during this period, she confided to us not long before she died that 'certain pressures had been applied' regarding the direction that others wanted her book to take. I'm especially glad that the two had the opportunity to make their peace before we lost Georgina.

But as for Charles's referring audience members to Georgina's book? Let me ask you, what accounts for someone directing you to a specific information source when they have to know the

Halt in Woodbridge

information you will find there will only discredit them? I don't have an answer for this, but it's exactly the case here. If you own a copy of *You Can't Tell the People*, go to the "Examining the Cause" chapter, then to page 32. The relevant sentence begins, "American researcher Peter Robbins speculates that some type of cloudbusting experiment may have been the cause of..." and goes on from there. Nowhere in this chapter or in this book will you find any reference to Charles's version of the 'cloud buster' or to Karl's dummy missiles.

Georgina Bruni did not think much of Col. Halt as a credible information source, this being something she made clear in a number of conversations we had at that time. Of course my saying this constitutes only hearsay, even if you take me at my word. However, Georgina sent me the following email on 29 September 1998. At the time I was employed by a multimedia corporation in Midtown Manhattan. I know that my former employers were meticulous record keepers and I expect the authenticity of this email could be confirmed with their cooperation. Two brief sentences have been removed as they were of a purely personal nature and have no bearing on the matter at hand:

Chapter 9: "They Talk About Cloud Busters"

Date: Tue, 29 Sep 1998 01:52:50 +0100

To: Peter Robbins <probbins@teamcpm.com>

From: georgina@easynet.co.uk

Subject: Re: HOT GOSSIP UK - SEPT

Hi Peter. Good news!!!!! I got the book deal with a nice advance too. It's being published by Sidgwick & Jackson - Macmillan. Signing next week. You are one of the first to know. I'd be honoured to be mentioned on your site Peter, and I'll russle up a brief thingie. How many words do you want? Thanks for answering those questions. Hope Larry is well. Please tell him about my book deal and the fact that my research has uncovered enough to completely confirm that he was there. It's not looking good for Halt though. Hugs, Georgina

Photo of one of Karl's dummy missiles or 'cloud busters' as they were then referred to according to Charles Halt, near RAF Bentwaters flight line. Photo: Larry Warren.

Finally, no 'dummy missiles,' made by Karl or by anyone else were deployed on the base earlier than 1983. I trust my source for this absolutely and invite anyone who served at Bentwaters in the early Nineteen Eighties who would like to confirm or dispute this to contact me. Larry Warren took the above photo of one of Karl's dummy missiles in 1985.

99

Weapon Storage Area, they said this is where certain weapons were kept, well that's...yes, that's where we kept the weapons, yes, so to speak. The forty eight A-10s with depleted uranium ammunition were in them.

To begin with, the image projected on the screen when the above statement was made is not the RAF Bentwaters Weapons Storage Area (WSA). But yes, "they" most definitely said that this was were "certain" weapons were stored, and with good cause. Because they were. Even so, the former deputy base commander suggests that because A-10s fire shells with depleted uranium in them, it was this weaponry and the aircraft themselves which were kept in *the* Weapons Storage Area. I fully respect the colonel's decision to hold to his National Security Oath and not confirm (or deny) the presence of nukes on base when he served there, especially as housing that stockpile was in violation of America's treaty with Great Britain at the time. This does not change the fact that the largest backline stockpile of American nuclear ordinance in England was stored at the Twin Base Complex.

The 'Hot Row,' RAF Bentwaters (nuclear) Weapons Storage Area. Photo: Peter Robbins.

Chapter 9: "They Talk About Cloud Busters"

These hardened bunkers define a narrow alley that was better known as the 'Hot Row.' Few base personnel were ever allowed in the double barbed wire-ringed enclosure that surrounded them or behind the massive sliding doors that opened on to the Hot Row. The photo below was taken from the WSA's observation tower and gives a better idea of how relatively small the actual enclosure really is. I'm not very good at estimating acreage but the entire WSA only extends out a hundred feet or so beyond the earthen covered structures to the right You can see for yourself how the far perimeter is defined by the road just before the tree line in the distance, and along the road that runs off to the left.

WSA from the observation tower. Photo: Peter Robbins.

Photo: Peter Robbins.

Halt in Woodbridge

An A-10 'Tankbuster' aircraft.

In this final Weapons Storage Area photo, you can make out the back fencing just beyond the tower. Even if the formidable A-10s had the ability to land, Harrier Jump-Jet style, within the confines of this modest-sized area, it would be sheer madness to attempt to do so among the hardened bunkers and prevalent utility poles. I don't know how the colonel managed to keep a straight face as he passed this fantasy off as fact to those who had paid their twenty pounds to hear him speak.

In the words of the American television jurist, Judge Judy, "Don't pee on my leg and tell me it's raining." Then again, a former deputy base commander would be far more knowledgeable than a civilian like me in such matters: "Yes, that's where we kept the weapons, yes, so to speak."

Chapter 10:
Halt and Hopkins

They talked to Budd Hopkins. Many of you probably know Budd Hopkins. Budd Hopkins and I became good friends. In fact, my wife and I were houseguests several times with him, and he had actually interviewed Larry Warren and regressed him. And his comment to me was "screen memories, induced memories." were the terms he used.

I can substantiate everything I've told you tonight, and I'm going to leave some copies of everything.

"He (the colonel) stated quite firmly that Larry was in no way forward of the service road and mentioned that Budd Hopkins had emphatically stated that his interviews with Larry indicated that his account was untrue." —David Bryant, 'Halt Briefing' Master of Ceremonies, 11 July 2015

No matter how "firmly" the colonel stated this, Security Specialist Warren was most definitely ordered to proceed "forward of the service road." And no matter how "emphatically" he would like us to believe that Budd Hopkins "indicated that his (Larry's) account was untrue," it's Mr. Halt's account that proves to be the fabrication.

Charles says that the authors of *Left At East Gate* "spoke with Budd Hopkins." This is true, though his wording suggests that contact between the authors and Hopkins was minimal at best. On the other hand, Mr. Halt characterizes his relationship with the well-known author-investigator-painter as their having become "good friends," to such a degree that he and his wife were Hopkins' houseguests several times.

Halt in Woodbridge

I know for sure that the colonel and his wife were Budd's houseguests at least once because I was directly responsible for it. Some years back when we were trying to come up with a new guest speaker for our-then long-running Intruders Foundation seminar series, I suggested that we consider bringing Mr. Halt to NYC from his home in Virginia. Budd liked the idea and it happened. How did I come into the picture when presumably I had only "talked" to the man? Because Budd Hopkins was one of my closest friends and most trusted colleagues for just under thirty-five years. I worked as his assistant for a good portion of that time, answered thousands (yes, thousands) of the letters he received with handwritten notes, was trusted with extremely confidential personal information about many of the hundreds of abductees he worked with, and was a major confidant of his as he was of mine. I was also a founding member of his Intruders Foundation and sat on its Executive Board.

Budd Hopkins and Peter Robbins in Hopkins's Lower Manhattan studio in 1994. Photo by New York Times staff photographer.

Chapter 10: Halt and Hopkins

Considering Halt's "good friends" characterization, you should have some insight into the turn this 'relationship' took once Budd was no longer around to defend himself against an extremely destructive action undertaken by his 'good friend.' Does this bear directly on the colonel's attempt to convince his audience that Hopkins believed Warren's account untrue? Oh yes, and it also 'goes to motive,' as they say in the courtroom dramas.

Prior to Budd's meeting the colonel at a UFO conference they were both speaking at, he only knew of the man via Larry's and my references to him in *Left At East Gate*. In 2008 or 2009, Budd was reintroduced to him through his close friend and colleague, the journalist Leslie Kean. She had included a chapter co-written by Halt in her book, *UFOs: Generals, Pilots and Government Officials Go On the Record*. I understand that the friendship that had existed between them has since been ended by her.

At Budd's request, all of his records, files, witness drawings, audiocassette recordings of hypnotic regressions and interviews (about twelve hundred or so as I recall), and the thousands upon thousands of letters that had been sent to him, were packed up and transferred to the home of his closest friend and colleague, Dr. David Jacobs, an Associate Professor of History at Temple University in Philadelphia and another noted UFO abduction researcher and author.

Only the people closest to Hopkins knew where these extremely confidential materials had been transferred to. For reasons best known to himself, Mr. Halt had decided he wanted to hear for himself the actual recording of the regressive hypnosis Warren had undergone with Hopkins and asked Leslie if she knew where it might be found, which was how Halt approached Jacobs about it. But given that Jacobs, like Hopkins, always protected the confidentiality of the many individuals he had worked with, how could Halt have possibly have acquired a copy of the tape?

Halt in Woodbridge

About two years ago, I found myself rereading the transcription of Larry's regression with Budd. There was one important detail I had deliberately withheld from the published transcription, and in the years since transcribing it, had forgotten the specifics of what it was. Here is Larry Warren on 15 July 1995 in hypnotic regression, a nineteen-year old airman again, with Budd Hopkins:

> LW. [Pause] And then another person comes in... Air Force, um... full colonel! "Airman Warren," uh, "come with me and sit in this other room." There's another room across the hallway from this. We go past these curtains, these partitions... to a hallway, cross the hallway is a, room... uh, Bustinza's sitting there: "How you doing?" We both... "How are you? What's..." just, numb. And, there's [Larry names four individuals] ... a lot of people I know.
>
> BH. Um hum. How many would you say in all?
>
> LW. Seven.
>
> BH. Um hum. And everybody's sitting down?
>
> LW. Yeah [pause], and... there's something wrong with this. [long pause] There, there is, a meeting! Uh...
>
> BH. Um hum.
>
> LW. ...but this is not the same, situation here [as the debriefing earlier in the day], um... [long pause] This, a... I'd like to jump out of this mode, I think. I think I really, would like to! This is um, this isn't right.
>
> BH. Larry, would you like to end this right now?
>
> LW. Yeah, I think so, oh I would...
>
> BH. Okay, we'll come back another time.
>
> LW. ...I would. I really would.
>
> BH. Okay... [Budd begins to bring Larry out. End of this regression.]
>
> (*LAEG*, pages 384-285)

When Larry identified Adrian and four of the other witness in that room, Budd and I looked at each other in something approaching shock. We talked with Larry about this completely unexpected turn of events once he had come out from under his

Chapter 10: Halt and Hopkins

hypnotic state, all of us appreciating the implications of what we had stumbled into. Given how the incident had begun in the parking lot with Adrian in clear view, and considering the other connections to his and Larry's shared experiences in the underground, we made the decision to keep his name in the published transcription—but not those of the other men. The most sobering issue we faced was in considering if any of them actually remembered this event or if they'd been blocked from doing so in some manner. Should we contact them about this and risk destroying their peace of mind if they were oblivious to it? No, we all agreed, and we should most definitely not include their names in the transcript either.

And so I made had made it my business to forget who they were, not that difficult to do, and continued on with my work. The upshot of this was a published transcription that was to-the-letter perfect, minus those four names. This redaction is not hidden in *Left At East Gate,* but the reader never learns who the men are. Rereading that part of our book eighteen years after the fact peaked my curiosity again. I called Larry in Liverpool to learn that he didn't remember the names either, but was also curious to relearn who they were.

Larry was fine about my requesting a copy of the tape from Dr. Jacobs so that we might resolve the matter and I phoned David at his home shortly afterward. He told me he's be glad to make and send me a copy, but a small formality had to be attended to first. The abduction researcher had his own strict set of protocols and needed a written, if brief, okay from Larry before duplicating the audiocassette. He asked me to let Larry know this and shortly thereafter my co-author fired off the following email to him:

> "Hi David, its been a long time. Peter told me to contact you, re, Budd's tape with me concerning Rendlesham, etc. And indeed I give you permission to release it, and use it in any way. Also I extend same to Peter Robbins. Wishing you and yours all the very best. Larry Warren"

David filed the email in the appropriate manila folder and sent me a copy of the tape. I listened to it, then shared the names of the men with Larry. The email itself was returned to its folder, and that's where it stayed until Charles Halt came calling last autumn. The colonel, whom he had never met, had sent Dr. Jacobs an email of his own requesting a copy of the tape for himself. Surprised that anyone other than the person involved would make such a request, the author/investigator went back to that file and found Larry's permission statement which included the unambiguous phrase that he and David and I all came to quickly regret: *"use it in any way."* These were the things Dr. Jacobs knew about the colonel at that time: he had contributed a chapter to Leslie Kean's book, he had been Larry's deputy base commander, he had been a guest speaker at an Intruders Foundation seminar, and that he had stayed at Budd's overnight following his presentation. With Warren's clearly-worded *"use it in any way"* blanket permission on file and no reason to expect subterfuge, Jacobs made and sent the colonel a copy, something he has regretted doing ever since I told him how it had been used.

Jacobs told me that no one in his, and we'd wager Budd Hopkins's, experience had *ever* given such blanket permission for usage of such a recording and we both agreed that Larry's doing so was only a mark of his openness and honesty. But why would Charles want a copy of the tape? There's no question that he would have read the transcription in his copy of *Left At East Gate*. This leaves me with only three possible reasons. The first, to learn for himself if I had dropped, altered or otherwise changed any part when transposing it into written form. If so he could accuse me of dishonesty in hiding or changing the content. If this was his intention he must have been sorely disappointed. Two, was there anything above and beyond the written words that he might learn about and use against Larry? And three, to learn the names of the four men Larry encountered in the underground, names which were absolutely none of his damned business. He may have been their superior officer thirty-plus years earlier, but he sure wasn't now.

Halt followed up with several emails to Dr. Jacobs and a call or two to see what he might learn from David about Larry. Jacobs, as open and honest in his way as Warren was in his, and unaware of Charles's long-term agenda, told the retired Air Force officer a number of things which he felt he had no reason to hide. Among them, that I had told him and Budd *more than a quarter century earlier,* that I was concerned that Larry was drinking and possibly taking drugs to deal with his PTSD, a syndrome both Jacobs and Hopkins were more than familiar with as it applied to some traumatized UFO abductees as well. David also shared some of his memories of a 1984 MUFON meeting, the first event of its kind that Warren had attended, and how frustrated and angry he seemed after speaking about what had happened to him. In December of last year Mr. Halt was a guest on two radio programs and used some of his time to 'interpret' what he had managed to learn from David Jacobs. Here are some of the remarks he made during the December 10, 2014 broadcast of Martin Willis's Podcast on Dark Matters Radio, first night witness John Burroughs also a guest on that show:

CH: (Larry) "has been used as a disinformation patsy."

CH: (Larry) "picked up stories from other people."

CH: "a story so ridiculous that nobody believes it, except Peter Robbins maybe. I know that he knows the truth too."

CH: The only other one out there is Larry Warren, and I have some pretty strong evidence now..

MW: Okay..

CH: ..that I'm not gunna put out on the air.

MW: Alright.

CH: It doesn't affect them (referring to Jim Penniston and John Burroughs).

MW: Ah, now Larry was not, a, he was only there for something like four weeks, ahead of time?

CH: Something like that. I don't have the exact dates in front of me.

CH: And would someone who was only there for four weeks have the ability to go off base..

CH: If they were taken or ordered off base, yeah. A question I have for him is how he got his airbase ground defense training, and all the necessary training from the time that he arrived, and posted on flight. It certainly is possible..

JB: I think it would really help if we could all get together, and bury the hatchet, and..

CH: I'm very willing to do it. I don't want to deal with Larry Warren anymore though. I know enough about what he did and what's wrong with the book (*LAEG*) and everything else, I have some sworn statements in writing that are very, interesting. ...

JB: Do you believe everything he says is false, is that what you're trying to say?

CH: No. No. He picked up stories from other people.

JB: Do you believe that he was messed with though.

CH: Definitely.

JB: Than why would they mess with him if he did not have some kind of involvement?

CH: Because they found somebody they could play and (inaud) and put out a good story.

(question about how Adrian Bustinza could have been with both Halt's team and next to Larry. John responds that Adrian says he saw Larry out there and was with him at one point.)

CH: Larry has some serious substance problems including multiple ones according to friends who know him well.

A few days after this Charles was Jimmy Church's guest on his great "Fade To Black" program and added to the remarks he'd made on Willis's show, including his knowledge that Larry Warren was a "drug addict." During both broadcasts he referred to Budd Hopkins as "my very good friend," though in reality he was not much of a friend at all.

During both broadcasts Halt let the listening audience know he had an actual copy of Larry's hypnotic regress with Budd –

Chapter 10: Halt and Hopkins

without ever telling them how he'd acquired it. This led many listeners to assume the tape had come from Hopkins himself. Has this been the case it would have constituted a career-ending lapse in professional ethics on Budd's part, but that is just want many listeners assumed, especially with the pioneer UFO abduction researcher no longer able to defend himself against the insinuation. As Budd Hopkins' longtime assistant, it was I who began receiving the calls, emails, and Facebook messages in the final days of December from some of the extremely concerned, angry and troubled abductees, experiencers and UFO witnesses Budd had worked with over the decades. David Jacobs helped me to sort out what had really happened and I did the same with those who contacted me.

This is David [referring to an image on the screen] – Doctor David Jacobs, former professor at Temple University who's very well known in the abduction field. He's written many books, and he was a partner to Budd Hopkins. In fact, he inherited all Budd Hopkins files. What he says:

(Reading) **"I was the MC of the UFO conference in Massachusetts around 1986 (unclear) all the research – doing a lousy job of research, not only of Bentwaters, but his personal experiences. He went on to say how he'd been kidnapped, taken to some sort of room underground and...let's see...various things had been done to him. I told him [Jacobs told Warren] he had to be very careful (unclear). He later admitted that he was lying."** That's Doctor David Jacobs.

Here is Doctor David Jacobs again.

(Reading) **"Larry Warren said to me Bustinza was reluctant to go public."** Which was true. Adrian Bustinza who was with me, the staff sergeant, was looking to get out of the service and he wanted to get a government job primarily in the southwest, near home. That would require security clearance and he wanted nothing to do with the UFO so he

did not want his name mentioned or want anything to do with it. So (resumes reading): "Larry thought he should adopt Adrian Bustinza's story as his."

The MUFON meeting David was chairing actually took place in Beverly Massachusetts in 1984. All things considered, how was Larry doing at about that time? Not very well:

> "My anger was changing me. I remembered the younger Larry as a nicer guy; now I was anything but. I justified the change as necessary; I had to be tougher as attacks on me continued. My real fear was of some government reprisal. But I didn't talk about it, sliding into a lethal depression, and found solace in the bottle more often than I cared to admit. I never really slept well anymore and dreamed of Bentwaters and the underground facility often" (*LAEG*, page 126)

Larry had been invited to give his account at that MUFON meeting. He talked about what he'd witnessed and experienced or been led to believe he'd experienced, including the underground and having been 'kidnapped,' as Halt characterized it. And kidnapped was an accurate way to describe being chemically subdued and taken someplace against your will. Warren did criticize, and with real emotion, the audience of researchers and investigators for not making it their business to investigate the RFI, though it had become public knowledge thirteen months earlier. The fact remained though that up until that evening it's likely no one in that audience had ever heard an account like this before or even knew how to react to it.

Yes, Larry, angry and frustrated, behaved in an anti-social manner before the group who, representative of the major thinking in ufology at the time, would still have had their attention focused on lights in the night sky, landing trace cases, radar reports and statistics and the like with no real way of wrapping their heads around the account they'd just hard. Given the unrelenting PTSD-induced pressures and dreams Warren was living with on a day-to-day basis, concerns for his family's privacy, his own safety, and for his own abilities to get serious word out about what had happened to him and others without becoming an object of ridicule and the uninformed judgements of others, is it any wonder he behaved as he did?

UFO group attempts to enlighten public

By ANDREA ATKINS
Times staff

BEVERLY — On Dec. 28, 1980, Art Wallace, an American Air Force security officer, was ordered into the woods near a British air force base where he observed animals running frenzied from the forest's interior.

As he and several colleagues searched the area, they saw light rays coming through the woods, heard helicopter sounds and observed what he described as a "transparent aspirin with a mist in the middle."

That Woodbrige, England, incident was the focus of conversation yesterday at the 2 Cherry Road home of Marge Christensen. Mrs. Christensen, a teacher at Beverly High School, has been involved in UFO investigations since she heard a lecture on UFOs about 10 years ago.

The meeting at her home was a regular session of the regional Mutual UFO Network Inc. About a dozen people attended, some from as far away as New York.

Larry Fawcett, one of the directors of the Mutual UFO Network, told the group that, according to the reports, "over the pine trees came a red ball which then burst into multi-colors. Where the aspirin was, there was a machine — triangular in shape, with lights on it."

After more than one hour's discussion of that day's events, Fawcett introduced Art Wallace (an assumed name) — the man who witnessed the incident.

Wallace said he has gotten accustomed to skepticism about his incredible story while at the same time he has undergone "unending harassment" from the military. "I know I wasn't crazy. I know it happened. I know it's hard for people to accept," said the 22-year-old New York state native who said he also saw three-foot tall beings that same night.

Fawcett and Mrs. Christensen are part of the Mutual UFO Network, an international scientific organization, which researches UFO sitings and tries to bring the information to the public.

They said yesterday that Wallace's sitting is significant because two days after it occurred, British researchers, none of whom knew the American Wallace, were told the same story about what went on in the woods near Woodbrugh.

UFO, page A8

• UFO sitings discussed

Continued from page 1

Dot Street, one of the British researchers, was at yesterday's meeting.

Ms. Street said she has been to the British Defense Ministry, the Forestry Ministry and other national departments with little success in learning the details of that December night.

She did learn, however, that the British Broadcasting Co. was told by the Forestry Department that something did happen in those woods, but "we've been told by the military not to say what."

And a letter obtained from U.S. Air Force Col. Charles I. Halt, confirms the incident.

"Early in the morning of 27 Dec. 1980, two USAF security police patrolmen saw unusual lights outside the back gate at RAF Woodbridge," Halt wrote in a Jan. 1981 memo to the RAF.

"The individuals reported seeing a strange glowing object in the forest. The object was described as being metallic in appearance and triangular in shape, approximately two to three meters across the base and approximately two meters high. It illuminated the entire forest with a white light. The object itself had a pulsing red light on top and a bank(s) of blue lights underneath. The object was hovering or on legs," Halt wrote.

The next day, the colonel reported, depressions were found in the forest floor.

The Mutual UFO Network (MUFON) wants to release more of the information it feels the government is withholding on this and other sitings. According to Ray Fowler of Wenham, the author of five books on the subject, and a member of MUFON, the government has no defenses against alien invaders and also fears the information gleaned from these sitings could be used against this country militarily.

"The United State might want to use this information to apply to its own weapons systems. They don't look at this from a scientific standpoint, but as a military issue," he said.

Wallace said he was ordered by his superiors to "keep quiet" about the incident and discovered a telephone call to his mother had been tapped and disconnected when he began to tell her the story.

He was until recently denied re-enlistment in the military. The incident, he said, has changed his life, made him wary of phone calls and talking with the media. He said his family worries about his safety.

But he is even angrier with people who attempt to dismiss what he claims he saw.

"There were people in England who said it was a lighthouse. It makes me sick. The human race is so derogatory to themselves when they say things like that. I never believed in this before, but when I saw it, I wanted to tell everyone about it," he said.

The Beverly Times article on the November 1984 MUFON meeting. Note: The staff reporter assigned to cover the meeting was obviously new enough to the subject that she confused or misunderstood the phrase 'UFO sightings' with embarrassing results.

I told him he had to be very careful (unclear). He later admitted that he was lying [quoting Dr. Jacobs]

David Jacobs *did* take Warren's account seriously, and in telling this unique witness "to be very careful," he was expressing his genuine concern for what might happen to him if he didn't. Equally important, Larry Warren *never* told David Jacobs that he was "lying" and Jacobs never once used the word in any exchange with Halt, of this he was absolutely certain. Once again, 'Larry changed his story' is transposed into "he was lying," then putting those words in the mouth of someone who had never said or written them. What Warren *did* share with Jacobs was how he and Bustinza had agreed that he should tell that part of their shared story as if it had happened to "a guy I knew" rather than to himself. Given the hoops I put myself through earlier in laying all this out for the reader, it any wonder that Jacobs, like Fawcett and Greenwood years earlier, came away not quite sure what to make of this young man?

During our last phone conversation in August, Dr. Jacobs asked me to share this message with you. He has *had* it with the quagmire known as the Rendlesham Forest UFO incident and would like nothing further to do with it in future. He is doing his best in getting back to living his life following the death of his beloved wife earlier this year. He is also starting to speak about his first new book in years, *Walking Among Us,* which I'm very much looking forward to reading. I ask that you honor his request and leave him alone regarding the RFI.

There remains this question though. What was Budd Hopkins' *actual* opinion of Larry Warren, the credibility of his account, and of the book *Left At East Gate*? From the beginning of my writing partnership with Larry, Budd was my confidant in all matters relating to Rendlesham. I worked for him throughout this period as well as prior to and following. Hopkins' name comes up more than thirty times in our book and anyone familiar with the man's reputation, professional integrity and published writings knows he would have never have lent his name to the kind of book Charles Halt wants you to believe my co-author and I wrote.

Chapter 10: Halt and Hopkins

Budd and Peter in 1997, the year "Left At East Gate" was first published. From the cover of issue 5 of the IF Bulletin. Photographer: I'm damned if I remember.

Here's what Budd Hopkins had say about our completed manuscript in 1996:

> "This is a powerful and compelling book. For me, its implicit central theme is the authors' personal courage and relentless search for truth in the face of official deception and attempts at direct intimidation. Warren and Robbins' narrative has the force of a well-told mystery novel, yet it is all disturbingly true. A major contribution to the literature."

The forward to the first edition of *Left At East Gate* was written by Anthony Grey, a former foreign correspondent with Reuters in Eastern Europe and China and author of the internationally bestselling historic novels, *Saigon, Peking, and Tokyo*. When I asked Budd if he'd be interested in writing a Forward to the second edition he told me he's be honored. Here are two excerpts from that Forward:

115

"In their detailed study of the UFO events at two adjoining British airbases, Bentwaters and Woodbridge, in late 1980, we find the highly personal voice of Larry Warren, an actual participant in both the encounters themselves and their subsequent cover-up, in tandem with the more detached, objective words of the veteran UFO investigator Peter Robbins. An attentive reader cannot escape either the legitimate emotions of the witness or the investigator's clear, rational search for truth. *Left At East Gate* is a complex book. In its pages, Larry Warren vividly describes his battles with personal demons, some typical of the nineteen-year old late adolescent that he was at the time, and others that followed his attempts to come to grips with an unimaginable and oppressive series of events. After his UFO encounter, more conflicts followed young Warren, a combination of the pressures he was subjected to by officials of the cover-up and his slowly deepening need, in spite of the risks, to go public with his experiences. His bravery in the face of direct and indirect threats becomes vividly apparent in *Left At East Gate*.

For his part, Peter Robbins smoothly describes the origins of his interest in the Bentwaters-Woodbridge UFO events, his first meeting with Larry Warren, and the difficult, rocky path these temperamentally disparate men followed in telling the story of *Left At East Gate*, Robbins' accounts of their joint visits to the original sites, and the uneasiness he felt as he tramped through the ominous fields, suggest the way in which an outside investigator can become enmeshed in the emotional reactions of the witness, vicariously sharing his state of mind. ...

In the interest of full disclosure the reader should know at the outset that I am personally well acquainted with both Larry Warren and Peter Robbins. As the two authors describe in *Left At East Gate*, in 1995 I conducted a hypnotic regression with Larry Warren as well as a number of probing conversations about his experiences, as well as an enlightening telephone interview with his mother. Peter Robbins I have known for more than twenty years. Not only has he assisted me in handling the voluminous and sensitive office correspondence I have received from UFO experiencers, but we have also worked well together on various field investigations; thus I know first-hand the intelligence and objectivity he has brought to his investigation into the incidents at Bentwaters. I am aware that to some, this familiarity may disqualify me as an objective commentator on *Left At East Gate*. However, to others, it may be seen as adding greatly to my understanding of Larry Warren and his role in this extraordinary case, and Peter Robbins's essential competence and investigatory skills. Between the two points of view, of course, the choice is yours to make. ...

As *Left At East Gate* amply demonstrates, the official policy seems to be to silence witnesses, to explain nothing, and to deny everything – even when UFO incursions take place at an Air Force base and adversely affected American personnel stationed there. In their jointly written book, Larry Warren and Peter Robbins have given us a truly disturbing account of the freedom with which UFOs and their crews can operate – and what may even be worse, the apparent helplessness and deceit of those whom we look to protect us."

Budd and Peter, August 2010.

And for the record, this is the inscription in my copy of Budd's book, *Witnessed: The True Story of the Brooklyn Bridge UFO Abductions*, published in 1996:

For Peter, a dear friend, an esteemed colleague, and a man to whom I feel enormous gratitude. You've done such great work with IF, with me, and with your own work on Bentwaters. I am in your debt – and I appreciate the wonderful humor. May there be many more great years for both of us. Budd Hopkins

Halt in Woodbridge

I apologize for this digression, but think the insights it offered give a deeper appreciation of the lengths which Mr. Halt has gone to in his quest to undermine the credibility of Larry Warren and the information contained in our book. I also felt it was particularly important in setting the record straight about Budd Hopkins and the recording that ended up in the colonel's hands.

Chapter 11:

On Being 'Meddled' With and a Certain Suicide

Many times I talked to Larry Warren trying keep him on track 'cause I wanted the book to come out and I wanted it to be right, and just got beat up every time, but he did admit many times that he'd been meddled with. We all knew that. He'd been drugged and hypnotised.

Charles Halt talked with Larry on a few – stress *few*, occasions over the years, and our book did come out "right." "Meddled with?" Definitely, and not unlike other witnesses such as John Burroughs, Adrian Bustinza, Ed Cavanasac and others, named and unnamed, who were put through variations of the same kind of mind-altering techniques that Larry Warren was. In *Encounter In the Rendlesham Forest* (published in 2014) first night witness Jim Penniston writes about the at least fourteen 'debriefings' he remembers, several of which were administered by non-Air Force personnel and several of which involved injections of something we can only make educated guesses about. Ed Cavanasac, former 81st SPS member assigned to C Flight also remembers, this from a letter he wrote to Larry after reading *Left At East Gate*:

> "I was out in the forest with Burroughs, Penniston and Dule on the first night. I worked C Flight and remember you from shift changes. I liked your book and learned some things about the base that I only suspected. We got debriefed for hours also! And I know we got injections ... I think now more than ever we were not supposed to remember certain things. ...We were ... scared, Burroughs drew his weapon on it and we went blank. Someone was inside that damned thing, you could feel it. The UFO did come back the next two nights so you must have been on D Flight. Rumors? Bullshit. No one was talking. ... But it was not from Earth." (*LAEG*, page xxvi)

Halt in Woodbridge

While some variation on these things *may* have happened to Larry, he remembers no military hypnotic sessions, no injections of any kind, or any instances of being "drugged," other than when he was chemically subdued with the aerosol that was sprayed in his face, this despite what Mr. Halt is fond of saying to the contrary.

It's interesting and depressing to note that the kind of critical undermining which the colonel applied to Larry Warren for so many years expanded into downplaying and demeaning the roles played by other Rendlesham witnesses including John Burroughs, Jim Penniston, Adrian Bustinza, Greg Battram and others. There is no question that Halt's treatment of Burroughs and Bustinza has been particularly shabby. An example was the colonel saying Burroughs TOOK him to the wrong first night landing site, and that John had "made claims that were clearly wrong" (UFO Truth Magazine, October 2013). This was decades after the fact, and in a wooded area that has seen many changes since 1980. How could Halt state with such certainty that this is the case? John was *there* when it happened. Charles was not.

For far too long, the relationship between John Burroughs and Larry Warren was frankly awful, driven by mistrust and misunderstanding that was actively being stirred for a time by their former deputy base commander. This all ended last September when Warren and Burroughs were brought together during a small conference in Woodbridge. It had been organized by Gordon (Gordy) Goodger, a local man who with an ongoing interest in UFOs since he was young. Gordy has taken it upon himself, with the help of a small cadre of volunteers, to organize a series of events in Woodbridge over the years. He organized a brilliant one for Larry and me in 1997. It was held in the nearby City of Ipswich as a part of our month-long UK book tour. Last September Warren and Burroughs really gave themselves a chance to talk it, comparing many aspects of their experiences and putting together pieces of the puzzle that neither could have accomplished on his own. Thank you Gordy for giving them the opportunity to do so.

Another unfortunate by-product of the RFI has been that men involved in the incident were deliberately driven to take sides against each other. In reality they were brothers-in-arms, united by their shared experiences, and united by their inability to fully deal with them. They and other witnesses suffered terribly as a result of what their 'debriefers' put them through. The Post Traumatic Stress Disorder (PTSD) they suffer from is in many ways similar to that suffered by combat veterans. But these PTSD-affected veterans remain unacknowledged by the USAF, the United States government, or the Veteran's Administration (VA), with one glowing exception. Last year the VA awarded John Burroughs a medical pension due to health problems stemming directly from having been exposed to whatever it was that he and Jim Penniston confronted in the Rendlesham Forest on the first night of UFO activity. Of course the Veteran's Administration nor the Air Force will never acknowledge the exact cause.

One of the colonel's ongoing arguments against the credibility of the witnesses who were 'meddled with' is that they cannot be trusted to give accurate testimony on *anything* regarding their claims and accounts. In fact many of the actual memories that were tampered with have emerged with clarity, in part with the assistance of the responsible, professionally administered hypnotic regressions these men have undergone.

This brings us to a somewhat sensitive question. Is there any possibility that Charles Halt was 'meddled with?' He was a UFO witness, after all and a commanding officer. I don't think it's out of the question, but we have no actual evidence for either argument. The object he observed passed overhead at a distance and was not encountered on the ground, in itself a huge difference in Close Encounter classifications. I believe this kind of encounter would be of the least interest to those in the intelligence / military intelligence community who were tracking the events of December 1980. But a secondary question is more difficult to dismiss. Did the colonel experience 'missing time' at some point during the third night? This phenomenon was

Halt in Woodbridge

prevalent among the other RFI witnesses and a healthy percentage of UFO witnesses overall. It's my opinion that he did. How did I come to take this view?

Gary Heseltine is a retired West Yorkshire police detective with a longtime interest in the subject of UFOs. This is especially so with regard to police-UFO encounters and forensic evidence sometimes recovered in the wake of such events. Haseltine is also publisher of the online bimonthly, 'UFO Truth Magazine.' Since at least 2010 the former detective had been fairly close to the colonel. In fact he had spent years developing a screen play in collaboration with Mr. Halt based on his views and opinions about the RFI. All this ended the day after the latter's 11 July talk. To properly characterize it, Heseltine was disgusted by Halt's attack, especially his dragging Larry's ex-wives into his talk. And it was Gary who made me consider the possibility that Mr. Halt may have experienced missing time. The colonel has told him that following their aerial encounter in the forest, he and his men entered Capel Green, made their way through the far field behind the first, then come round the other way. Had the timing been right, this would have put the colonel and his men right in the line of sight of the event involving Warren, Bustinza, Ball, et al. But when Heseltine asked Halt what he actually saw at that moment, the colonel responded, and I quote, "That's the funny thing. I don't remember."

And again, in the interests of accuracy, my co-author never "beat up" Charles Halt, allegorically or otherwise, in any of the "many times I talked to Larry Warren trying keep him on track 'cause I wanted the book to come out and I wanted it to be right, and just got beat up every time."

He talks about somebody who committed suicide and went missing. At one point he says it was Alabama his roommate. Another time he says it was a cop who read the bible and different things. And he had problems, and he went AWOL to Chicago. We actually had somebody at that time frame

Chapter 11: On Being "Meddled" With and a Certain Suicide

who did do something like that. He didn't commit suicide. ...

The colonel continued on from here to describe an all-but-identical situation where another airman went AWOL (Absent Without Leave), but as noted, that airman did not take his life after being returned to the base. Let's review what Larry wrote about this tragic episode:

> "Many events followed in rapid succession. Some were tragic. One of the first odd things I noticed was that some of my fellow cops, ones who had seen the UFO, were suddenly no longer on base. The poor kid who'd read the Bible during the debriefing was so shook up about being told that religion had been invented to maintain order and control that soon after he went AWOL. He flew to Chicago, where he was met by the FBI, put on the next plane to England, and returned to duty. He'd told me he felt the place was evil and that, if he didn't get out, he'd die. Shortly thereafter, he blew his head off while on post. I saw the aftermath of the suicide, and it wasn't pleasant. People who didn't know the truth said he had been unstable to begin with; I knew otherwise. For the base commanders, the tragedy was just one more thing to cover up. For me, it was one more thing to expose."

Halt states as one of his many 'facts' that Larry Warren "talks about somebody who committed suicide and went missing [though obviously not in that order]. At one point he says it was Alabama his roommate. Another time he says it was a cop who read the bible and different things." In an attempt to shield the privacy of the family of the airman who took his life, Warren made the decision in to be purposely ambiguous about this young man's identity when writing about it in *Left At East Gate*. In fact 'Alabama' *was* the airman who went through the debriefing with a Bible in his lap praying quietly to himself throughout. He then went AWOL and the rest you know. Halt could have easily been forgiven for citing the confusion he felt, but used the opportunity in one more attempt to deceive his audience. He did so by crediting a single error that *I* had made, and on one occasion, but wording his query to sound as though

Larry was the culprit and not me. You should also be aware that the error was in no way associated with *Left At East Gate*, In fact it was from something I had written *seventeen years* after our book had been published.

This single glaring error – the only one I know of that got by me in *Deliberate Deception*, was incredibly embarrassing when I discovered it after the free online book had gone viral. The error never appeared anywhere else and will be corrected when I revise the text of that online book sometime this fall. Had the colonel been honest and said something like, 'In a book Peter Robbins wrote last year the airman who Larry Warren identified as the suicide was his roommate for a time and went by the nickname of 'Alabama.' Robbins then writes that it was the airman with the Bible in the debriefing. Which is it, and is Peter Robbins responsible for this confusion or is Larry Warren?' That would have been the appropriate way to handle it, but instead the audience is led to understand that Larry Warren once again appears to be confused by the facts of his own life. This 'error' on Halt's part could not have been accidental.

There was however the officer referred to earlier, the one who expressed such a serious interest in Warren's injuries. And it was him again who exhibited genuine concern over this airman's death. He also took Larry Warren's account as seriously as he did our book.

Peter Hill-Norton (Baron Hill-Norton) was a senior Royal Navy officer during the Second World War who rose to become Admiral of the Fleet (First Sea Lord, which was Britain's highest ranking Naval officer). He was named Chief of the Defence Staff of Her Majesty's Ministry of Defence in the early Nineteen Seventies and completed his service to his country as a Member of Parliament's (MP) House of Lords. Hill-Norton was nobody's fool, least of all Larry's and mine. He had followed developments in the Rendlesham Forest case from the first day's news coverage on. Not even he had an inkling of the RFI until the story broke in the News of the World in October of 1983, an

Chapter 11: On Being "Meddled" With and a Certain Suicide

Admiral Lord Peter Hill-Norton (8 February 1915 – 16 May 2004).

indication of how tightly locked down it had been. His opinions regarding almost all so-called UFO researchers and investigators were *not* good, and that is putting it mildly. But he did have great respect for the British author and researcher Timothy Good and even wrote the Introduction to Good's outstanding book, Above Top Secret.

Not surprisingly, the UFO incident that interested and concerned him the most occurred in Suffolk in December 1980. He followed developments in the story for the rest of his life and with a genuine passion. He made his first public statement about the RFI only six days after it became public knowledge: "I must speak out. The Ministry of Defence know far more than they are prepared to say. But now they have an obligation to tell the nation what occurred that night in a British wood." And the witness who interested him the most from October 1983 on was the whistle-blower airman first known as 'Art Wallace.'

News of the World headline featuring Hill-Norton's first public statement about the Rendlesham Forest incident in the paper's 9 October 1983 edition.

In 1993 Timothy Good was kind enough to arrange an introduction with Hill-Norton along with his phone number and a day and time he would be expecting us to call. We did so from a payphone outside our cheap London hotel during yet one more research trip to the UK. I spoke with him first, giving the MP a progress report on how our investigation was coming along, and asking him if he'd like to receive an uncorrected proof copy whenever it became available as well as the published version of *Left At East Gate*. No, he curtly responded. He only wanted to read the book once thank you and would wait until it was published. I then turned the receiver over to Larry who greeted Admiral Lord Hill-Norton with a big "Hi Pete," which quietly freaked me out. Larry's smile indicated that the greeting seemed well met and the two went on speaking for quite a while. It was during this call that Larry told Hill-Norton about the presence of the nuclear ordinance at RAF Bentwaters when he'd been stationed there, and in so many words, the MP hit the roof. Even in his position as a former MOD Chief of Staff he'd been unaware of this staggering treaty violation and spent a good part of his remaining years as England's highest ranking critic of excessive UFO secrecy, especially regarding a series of UFO incidents at an American nuclear base in Suffolk and the extremely dangerous implications of such a situation.

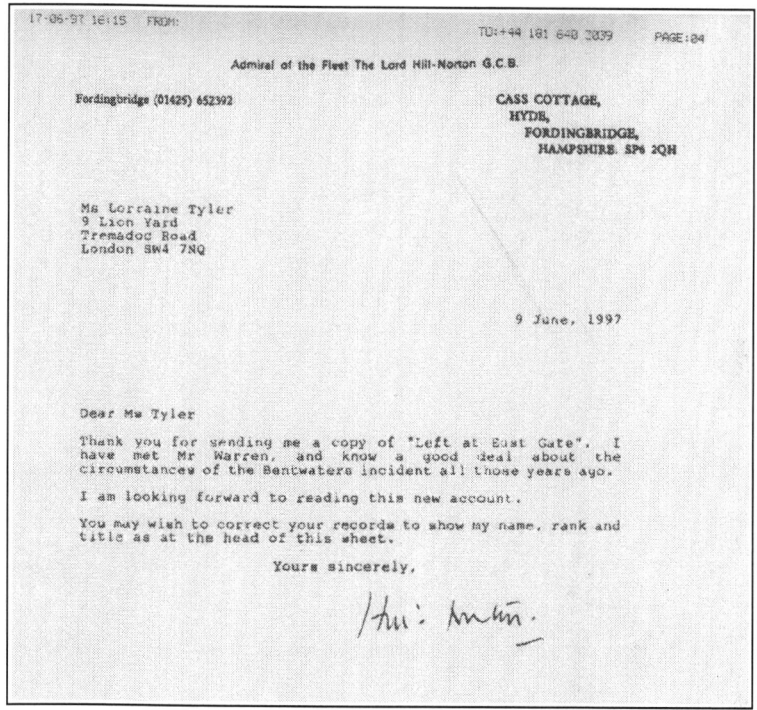

A 9 June 1997 letter from Lord Hill-Norton to our UK publicist Ms. Tyler at Michael O'Mara Books.

He was of course sent a copy of *Left At East Gate* as soon as it was available, as was the newly installed Prime Minister, Tony Blair. Several months later Hill-Norton did something quite extraordinary. On 28 October 1997 he walked onto the floor of the House of Lords, his copy of *Left At East Gate* in hand, and asked Lord Gilbert, the-then Secretary for Defence, a series of questions, all of which had been drawn directly from our book. These are the questions he asked along with Lord Gilbert's understandably circumspect answers:

127

Lord Hill-Norton: Whether the allegations contained in the recently published book *Left At East Gate* to the effect that nuclear weapons were stored at RAF Bentwaters in violation of the UK/US treaty obligations are true.

Lord Gilbert: It has always been the policy of this and previous governments neither to confirm nor deny where nuclear weapons are located either in the UK or elsewhere, in the past or at the present time. Such information would be withheld under Exemption 1 of the Code of Practice on Access to Government Information.

Lord Hill-Norton: Whether they are aware of reports from the United States Air Force personnel that nuclear weapons stored in the Weapons Storage Area at RAF Woodbridge were struck by beams fired from an unidentified craft seen over the base in the period 25-30 December 1980, and if so, what action was subsequently taken.

Lord Gilbert: There is no evidence to suggest that the Ministry of Defence received any such reports.

Lord Hill-Norton: What information they have on the suicide of the United States Security Policeman from the 81St Security Police Squadron who took his life at RAF Bentwaters in January 1981, and whether they will detail the involvement of the British Police, Coroner's office, and also other authorities concerned.

Lord Gilbert: MoD has no information concerning the alleged suicide. Investigations into such occurrences are carried out by the US Air Force.

Lord Hill-Norton: What information they have on the medical problems experienced by various United States Air Force personnel based at RAF Bentwaters and RAF Woodbridge, which stemmed from their involved in the so-called Rendlesham Forest incident, in December 1980.

Lord Gilbert: Information on medical matters relating to US personnel is a matter for the US authorities."

A few years back the Ministry of Defence made public (at least the unclassified portion) of their substantial file on Hill-Norton. This letter to Lord Gilbert was among the documents and letters the file contained: The two other letters that follow are from secretaries to Prime Minister Blair, the first is to our publisher, the second to a constituent who had written to the PM admonishing him to read our book:

And about the name of the airman who took his life, it is known to us, of course. However for the same reasons Larry withheld it from publication in 1997 and 2005, we do not include it here either. I trust you will take my word for this.

> **Written Answers**
>
> *Tuesday, 28th October 1997.*
>
> **Mr. Reginald Buckland: Court Documents**
>
> Lord Burton asked Her Majesty's Government:
>
> Whether they will place in the Library of the House a copy of the judgment delivered at Cambridge Crown Court on 11 September 1997, and all other papers and documents submitted to the court, in case A970014, the appeal of *Reginald Buckland v. The Chief Constable of Cambridge* before His Honour Judge Haworth heard on 15 August 1997 against the refusal of the Chief Constable to vary the conditions of a firearms certificate, and in particular all other papers, documents, disclosures and submissions which Mr. Robert Gardiner, Clerk to the Court, has failed to provide upon request by Lord Burton.
>
> The Lord Chancellor (Lord Irvine of Lairg): The Question concerns a matter which has been assigned to the Court Service under the terms of its Framework Document. I have therefore asked the Chief Executive to respond.
>
> *Letter to Lord Burton from the Chief Executive of the Court Service, Mr. M. D. Huebner, dated 28 October 1997.*
>
> RELEASE OF COURT DOCUMENTS
>
> The Lord Chancellor has asked me to reply to your Question about the release of papers and documents submitted to the court in the case of *Reginald Buckland v. The Chief Constable of Cambridge*.
>
> A copy of the judgment was placed in the Library of the House on 7 October. As the remaining documents are the property of the party who filed them, there is no obligation or authority for the court to disclose them. With Mr. Buckland's consent, copies of correspondence between himself and the respondent were provided to you on 15 October, and will today be placed in the Library.
>
> **Central and Eastern Europe: Military Training Assistance**
>
> The Earl of Carlisle asked Her Majesty's Government:
>
> How many individual service personnel and military training teams from the United Kingdom Armed Forces will be deployed throughout 1998, in the countries of Central and Eastern Europe which were formerly occupied by the Soviet Union, to assist with the training of their Armed Forces.
>
> The Minister of State, Ministry of Defence (Lord Gilbert): The Ministry of Defence currently expects to deploy six individual Service personnel and 10 military Short Term Training Teams to the countries of Central and Eastern Europe in 1998. All are deployed at the specific request of the countries concerned, who seek to benefit from the expertise of the United Kingdom's Armed Forces. The aim of the training teams is to advise on the conduct of either officer or non-commissioned officer training. The individual Service personnel, all officers, are deployed to provide expertise in specific areas of defence management.
>
> **RAF Bentwaters and Woodbridge: Nuclear Weapons Allegations**
>
> Lord Hill-Norton asked Her Majesty's Government:
>
> Whether the allegations contained in the recently published book *Left at East Gate*, to the effect that nuclear weapons were stored at RAF Bentwaters and RAF Woodbridge in violation of UK/US treaty obligations are true.
>
> Lord Gilbert: It has always been the policy of this and previous governments neither to confirm nor to deny where nuclear weapons are located either in the UK or elsewhere, in the past or at the present time. Such information would be withheld under exemption 1 of the Code of Practice on Access to Government Information.
>
> Lord Hill-Norton asked Her Majesty's Government:
>
> Whether they are aware of reports from the United States Air Force personnel that nuclear weapons stored in the Weapons Storage Area at RAF Woodbridge were struck by light beams fired from an unidentified craft seen over the base in the period 25–30 December 1980, and if so, what action was subsequently taken.
>
> Lord Gilbert: There is no evidence to suggest that the Ministry of Defence received any such reports.
>
> Lord Hill-Norton asked Her Majesty's Government:
>
> What information they have on the suicide of the United States security policeman from the 81st Security Police Squadron who took his life at RAF Bentwaters in January 1981, and whether they will detail the involvement of the British police, Coroner's Office, and any other authorities concerned.
>
> Lord Gilbert: MoD has no information concerning the alleged suicide. Investigations into such occurrences are carried out by the US Forces.
>
> Lord Hill-Norton asked Her Majesty's Government:
>
> What information they have on the medical problems experienced by various United States Air Force personnel based at RAF Bentwaters and RAF Woodbridge, which stemmed from their involvement in the so-called Rendlesham Forest incident, in December 1980.
>
> Lord Gilbert: Information on medical matters relating to US personnel is a matter for the US authorities.

The questions and responses Hill-Norton asked Lord Gilbert were all dutifully noted in Hansard's Official Report, an edited verbatim report of proceedings of both the House of Commons and the House of Lords. It is Parliament's equivalent of The American Congressional Daily Record.

Chapter 11: On Being "Meddled" With and a Certain Suicide

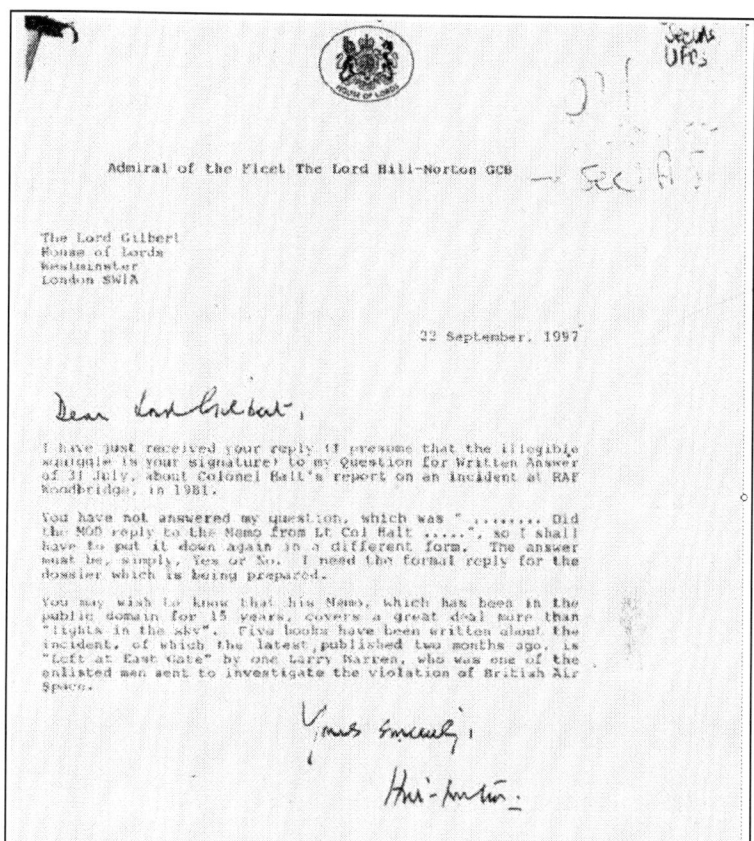

10 DOWNING STREET
LONDON SW1A 2AA

From the Assistant Private Secretary   9 June 1997

Dear Mrs. Tyler,

The Prime Minister has asked me to thank you for your letter of 5 June with which you kindly enclosed a review copy of *Left at East Gate* by Larry Warren and Peter Robbins.

Yours sincerely,

MRS. D.C. AILES

Ms Lorraine Tyler

Chapter 11: On Being "Meddled" With and a Certain Suicide

10 DOWNING STREET
LONDON SW1A 2AA

From the Assistant Private Secretary   20 September 1997

Dear Mr. Cave,

The Prime Minister has asked me to thank you for your letter of 20 August.

I regret that the Prime Minister has not yet had an opportunity to read *Left At East Gate*.

Yours sincerely,

Deborah Ailes

MRS DEBORAH AILES

Martin Cave Esq

Chapter 12:
Regarding Adrian Bustinza

Picked up the story from Adrian Bustinza apparently

No, Larry Warren didn't 'pick up' the story from Adrian Bustinza, "apparently" or otherwise. He *lived* a good part of it with him though. Early on Bustinza had made the decision to remain out of the Rendlesham debate to the greatest degree possible and who can blame him? But by the fall of 2013 he had had it with people saying Larry was not present on the third night. It was then he sent a message to a mutual friend, Ronnie Dugdale. Over the years Ronnie had become extremely knowledgeable about the RFI and Adrian gave him his permission to post the message on his Facebook page. This is part of that message, dated 21 October 2013:

> "They are all my Friends and I will defend them until the end of time because they were there with me and the experience was together. I know what I have said and yes I do remember. How could anyone forget those nights! They were all there at one point and another and I experienced those nights with them all. Brothers in Distress and Brothers for Life. *OK I will say this YES, YES Larry was there!* But so was John, and the rest of the guy's" (Emphasis mine).

...documentation on that...from some of the other cops...suddenly put himself into the story."

Charles claims to have documentation from some of the cops, presumably supporting his long-running allegation that Larry "put himself into the story." Very good. While we wait for him or someone else to allow us access to this 'documentation,' you can read these statements "from some of the other cops:"

Chapter 12: Regarding Adrian Bustinza

"It's real, it happened to us, and we will never forget it. Your book brought it all back for me. ... (How) Halt can put it all into a little box is beyond me. He should take at least some responsibility for helping to keep the lid on the thing! Oh sure, he talks about what he saw but what about the hell we went through afterward. Thanks for fighting for us Larry, I'm grateful. Now maybe we can all get a good night sleep."

—Mark Thompson, former 81st Security Police Specialist assigned to D Flight

"I know you were out in that forest cause I saw you out there, and we were all on duty with full PRP. Col. Halt should review the regs on posting. I just wish I knew why those things landed and what they wanted, isn't that the most important question? No light houses and theories from people who don't have a clue. I remember that call to the States that you made, then you were gone for a few days. Holy shit. I had no idea."

—Greg Battram, former 81st Security Police Specialist assigned to D Flight

"17 years blew by quick – I tried to forget the UFO, but Left At East Gate brought it all back! How can Halt play it down – you were there and so was I. We got debriefed after, and some guys like you got f**ked over later for asking too many questions. I remember that Navy guy saying that "bullets are cheap." The difference between us, I guess, is that I believed him. ... People died over this for God's sake. Maybe they were right when they told us that civilians were not ready for this yet. I will try and get in touch with other witnesses and let them know about East Gate."

—Another D Flight SP who prefers to have his name withheld for now.

At the time of the incidents Sergeant Adrian Bustinza was a C and D Flight Supervisor. He stood directly to Larry's right in Capel Green and is referred to on fifty two pages of *Left At East Gate*; thirty six in the narrative and another sixteen of interview transcription. Adrian wrote to Larry in 1997:

"No one can give us back what we lost over there. All people will do is rip us off and never understand the truth. ... Larry remember "duck and cover" cause your book is gonna set off a lot of powerful people that have a lot to lose if this gets out. I wish I didn't encourage you to go public, none of us knew what we were getting into, but I guess we never really had a choice. God bless and stay safe."

—From letters to Larry Warren, sent care of our American publisher in 1997. (LAEG, 2005 Cosimo Books edition, pages xxiv-xxv)

They were with me the whole time. Bustinza never left my side.

Yes, there is no question that Sgt. Bustinza and Sgt. Ball were with Col. Halt and the other men in his group throughout their shared UFO sighting in the forest. But following this, they were *not* with Col. Halt. They were in Capel Green with Larry Warren. A while back we reviewed the colonel's statement about security police not being assigned side arms (hand guns). Information that helped resolve this question was also included in Adrian's October 2013 message to Ronnie Dugdale:

> "I know who was with me at all three different times of one night [the third night] because I was instructed to go with certain guy's and to go pick-up certain lieutenants, sergeants, Yes I was all over the place because I was the NCOIC [Noncommissioned Officer In Charge] that night! That means that I could go anywhere and I did. Light All's units, Trucks, Fuel Depot, Field, communicating back and forth both verbally in person and over the Radio!"

I think the reason Sgt. Bustinza may have been authorized to carry a side arm as stated, was because he was the NCOIC that night.

There are four things, I am told, that substantiate Larry's story: Number One - my memo. Does anyone see his name anywhere in my memo? Number Two – my tape. Well that incriminates him because Bobby Ball who he claims was with him, and Sergeant Bustinza who claims was with him, was

with me there on the tape. Listen to the tape carefully. Bustinza's Security 10. And Bobby Ball was Security 4...or something...I don't know...but if anybody runs through the tape, and I've got copies in the narrative. They were with me the whole time.

Mr. Halt's "four things" one at a time, though I'm curious to know what the source of his "I am told" is. I've run out of ways to vary this phrase, but Larry Warren has never said, suggested or written that Charles Halt's memo of 13 January 1981 in any way acted to "substantiate" his involvement in the RFI. Why would he? Nothing in the document refers to him or confirms his involvement in the least.

The same can be said of "Number Two" and in the same terms. The so-called 'Halt tape' - that fifteen or so minute part of the recording many of us are now long familiar with from its wide use in TV programs, documentaries and radio shows. But as it in no way involved or referred to Warren, why would he ever say it substantiated his claim? More first rate nonsense.

Well that incriminates him because Bobby Ball who he claims was with him, and Sergeant Bustinza who claims was with him, was with me there on the tape. Listen to the tape carefully. Bustinza's Security Ten. And Bobby Ball was Security Four or something...

There is a very real problem here, but not the one the colonel refers to. Is Charles Halt prone to some profound mental block regarding time and place, or was he just hoping his audience might be? The logic applied here is identical to that used in arriving at two earlier 'findings,' 'There was no light on in the farmhouse when I observed it therefore a light couldn't have been on when Warren observed it later.' 'There were no cows in the field as Larry claims because there were no cows in the field

Halt in Woodbridge

when I was there earlier that night.' In this case, Bustinza and Ball were in the forest with the colonel during the group's now-famous UFO sighting, however the two sergeants could not have been in Capel Green with Warren later that night. That is what this excuse for an argument comes down to.

Bustinza never left my side. He was in shock and so frightened he stuck to me like wallpaper. I couldn't get rid of the guy. He was like this with me all the time. He was so nervous.

The statement above is a low point even for Mr. Halt. What kind of officer chooses to belittle a man under his command when that individual exhibits rational fear in a truly frightening situation – if indeed Sgt. Bustinza was as frightened as the colonel makes him out to be. Charles on the other hand seems to like presenting himself as the beleaguered standard-bearer of truth and objectivity in all things Rendlesham.

I have an email from Adrian Bustinza. Basically what it says is (paraphrasing), when I got back to the dormitory the first person I ran into – cos they were in the same dormitory - was Larry Warren. He said I had to tell somebody, so I told Larry my story.

Correction. Adiran Bustinza and Larry Warren lived two buildings away from each other. And I think all three of us would like to see the exact text of that email. Let's see how this really went down:

> "The last week of April I received my approval for honorable discharge; the date, May 18. One extremely foggy night, I found a note pushed under the door to my room. It was from Adrian. He wanted to talk; a time and place would be decided later. Celebrating at a barbecue, Bustinza told me to meet him in his room

that night. I got there about 10:00 P.M., and he threw his roommate out. The kid knew he was going to miss out on one hell of a conversation, but we couldn't take chances.

Adrian said he knew I was getting out sooner than he, and wanted me to have some facts before I left. He and others wanted the story out and felt I could get the ball rolling, and I agreed. He told me that Airman Burroughs had pictures of the UFO, and that a few others had other evidence. Adrian had been put through the wringer along with me, and he'd also found his loyalty to the Air Force faltering. He had also had earlier UFO experiences, and noted that some OSI agents on Bentwaters also had been at his last base -- a base with a high incidence of UFO activity.

We shared our thoughts about the underground base, and although I was unsure about what was real and what was imagined, he assured me the place existed and was an alien installation. My mind was blown.

Adrian went on to say that the airbases were just a front for such installations. But for what reason? "Go to the newspapers, TV -- do anything to get this out, Larry. The bastards have hurt too many of us to let them get away with it." I agreed; afterward, he cried and so did I. Then we shook on it. I opened the door to leave and five eavesdropping airmen fell into the room, just like a Marx Brothers movie. How would I get the story out? I didn't know, but decided there and then I'd commit every resource I had to force the truth out into the open. I wouldn't turn back!" (*LAEG.* pages 73-74)

While I don't share the belief Adrian held back then about the underground being an alien base (I think the presence is all-to-human), I wondered what his thoughts on this and other RFI matters were today. As it turned out I didn't have long to wait. A surprise announcement on Tuesday 25 August gave notice that Adrian C. Bustinza III would be giving his first radio interview in the thirty four-and-a-half years since he and Larry Warren stood together in that farmer's field.

The program, "Phenomenon Radio" on KGRA, was broadcast on 27 August. It was hosted by John Burroughs with investigative writer and documentary filmmaker Linda Moulton

Howe cohosting. Larry Warren was also a guest. I don't think there was any question in the minds of listeners that Adrian Bustinza showed real courage in finally taking his story to the public.

One of those listening was former Air Force Captain Robert Salas, no stranger to the subject of UFO cover-ups himself. His observant 28 August write-up of the radio show gives a fair idea of what Adrian had to say during this historic broadcast. It also sheds some additional light on Col. Halt's third night involvement:

> "Tonight, on the KGRA show Phenomenon, Adrian Bustinza, a key witness spoke out in detail about his RFI experience after over thirty years of essentially keeping quiet. At the end of his testimony he admitted that he had been silent out of fear for his life and the lives of others because of the threats he received during interrogations by AFOSI and other intelligence agents. Larry Warren, John Burroughs and Linda Moulton Howe participated in the discussion tonight.
>
> Confirmations
>
> Adrian was in the Rendlesham forest during the third night of the incidents. During the show, he confirmed the following:
>
> Larry Warren was definitely out there with he and John Burroughs, Col. Halt and many others.
>
> Col. Halt ordered him to confiscate any cameras/recorders by others in the field.
>
> Col. Halt was in constant contact with the base Command Post during the incident.
>
> He and Burroughs had a close encounter with a bright light overhead. During this encounter, he experienced a force field that first pushed him to the ground and then lifted him up.
>
> Both he and Warren encountered a yellow colored mist near the ground level. He also confirmed that lights came from this mist and seemed to form some type of being, confirming a similar statement that Larry Warren has made. His recollection is not clear on this point.

Chapter 12: Regarding Adrian Bustinza

He, Burroughs and Warren do not recall how they returned back to the base that night.

Afterwards he called home (U.S.) and spoke with his mother about the incident. She told him their house was being 'watched' by men in a government car. This statement was confirmed by his father during a later call. His parents felt intimidated because the father held a government job. They asked him to just cooperate with the agents.

Later, he was interrogated at length by OSI and other intelligence agents. During his interrogations he was threatened with death ("bullets are cheap") unless he told the story of the events the way they wanted it told. He was told to say that the lights were from the lighthouse in the distance. After at first resisting, he finally agreed out of fear for his life.

After the incident he was sent on many deployments on temporary duty in order to keep him and other witnesses from discussing the incident together.

He developed strange bumps on his skin and fungal infections. Doctors cannot determine cause of these but radiation exposure is suspected.

He had a previous UFO encounter over the flight line at Mather AFB (Sacramento, CA). During this fly-over by a large UFO of multi-colored lights, fully nuclear armed B-52's were parked on Alert by the flight line.

He confirmed that nuclear weapons were stored at Bentwaters Base (Woodbridge).

Some implications from his testimony (in my opinion)

Clearly the AFOSI and other intelligence agencies were involved in covering up the RFI by many means, including death threats. Other witnesses also report being drugged during interrogations. This testimony again confirms that a deliberate attempt at disinformation and cover-up was made of this incident by government agents. Of course this implies a highly secret organization exists for this purpose for this kinds of incidents.

By confirming that nukes were kept at the base during this incident and the nuclear bomber base at Mather during another

Halt in Woodbridge

UFO encounter, this testimony is more validation of the UFO/nukes connection.

His testimony validates one of the methods used at maintaining secrecy of such incidents. Witnesses are deliberately scattered to other assignments to keep them from discussing the incident among themselves and others on the base. I have also presented evidence of this technique.

Not least of all, he confirmed much of Larry Warren and John Burroughs testimonies about the incident. The fact that the stories of these three is becoming cohesive is a welcome sign that we may all get some closure as to the facts of the RFI. Of course it would be helpful if more of the witnesses came forward.

Adrian's testimony suggests more questions for Col. Halt

Col. (ret.) Charles Halt has been a visible witness to the RFI. He has testified during press conferences and UFO conferences. For some time, I have thought that Col. Halt has not been completely forthcoming with the facts of the RFI and his involvement. Adrian's testimony brings to mind some of the questions that, in my mind are still unanswered.

Why has Halt often declared that Larry Warren was not involved during the third night of the incident? Why has he made such a concerted effort to discredit Warren's testimony over the years?

Since he was the commanding officer in the field, why were there 30-50 other people out there that night? Surely, he would have been involved in directing all of those people. Why was he in constant contact with the Command Post? Was he being directed for some purpose?

Why did he order that all cameras and recorders be confiscated? This was supposed to be an investigation of strange lights. More photos would have helped such an investigation.

I have other questions too but these may be pursued at a later time.

During his recent presentation in Woodbridge, according to Peter Robbins and others, Halt made some highly questionable statements. Robbins has stated that he will soon publish a full accounting of what he considers discrepancies and untruths in

Halt's statements. I hope Halt will take the opportunity to respond to the above questions and Robbins inquiries.

It is high time there was more clarity about the RFI. Tonight, Mr. Adrian C. Bustinza III gave us more clarity and confirmation. I thank him for his courage and his testimony."

For your information, Robert Salas served on active duty with the U.S. Air Force for seven years after graduation from the U.S. Air Force Academy in 1964. He earned a Masters degree in Aerospace Engineering from the Air Force Institute of Technology, Wright-Patterson AFB, Ohio. He also worked with the Titan III Missile Systems program office at Los Angeles AFS. After being honorably discharged from the Air Force in 1971, Mr. Salas briefly worked as an engineer for Martin-Marietta Aerospace and Rockwell International. From 1974 until his retirement in 1995, he worked for the Federal Aviation Administration as an aircraft structures engineer. Robert Salas has authored two books on the UFO phenomenon: *Faded Giant* (2005) and *Unidentified - The UFO* Phenomenon (2014). He has spoken publicly about the 1967 UFO/Missile Shutdowns since 1996.

Chapter 13:

"Let's Talk About Soil Analysis"

The hill-field at Capel Green, where the UFO landed supposedly. Which no one else by the way can substantiate or verify.

There is no "hill-field" at Capel Green. It's a *field*. And as anyone familiar with that part of Suffolk knows, there are no hills in this area. But there are other men, dozens of them, who can verify the exact location where they were ordered to surround the strange ground fog, and where a UFO appeared soon afterward. Why haven't they all come forward and put themselves on the line shoulder-to-shoulder with Larry Warren? Reading this, do you really have to ask?

Let's talk about soil analysis. This is the good part.

The soil analysis - says the area was subjected to high energy or high heat, and the grass around the edge is very green. When I was growing up, my grandfather was an avid gardener and every fall he would burn a big pile of brush and (inaudible) and now and then he would take the ashes and put it round his lettuce and everything. One of the main ingredients of a fire like that is potash. Potash. Potassium. The third ingredient in fertilizer. Now, if you've ever had a brush fire, you can only get something around fourteen hundred fifteen hundred to two thousand degrees, and it stays hot for a long time. The sandy soil yes turned into almost glass. It was crystalized. What do you think did that? It wasn't radiation, it was heat. The farmer burns brush. All farmers' burn brush. Brush is a constant problem. Any time you leave the field sitting you know what happens. It makes things grow. If you don't keep ploughing and

Chapter 13: "Let's Talk About Soil Analysis"

moving…?...then it's a problem. So, one, two, three, four. Guess what? You're up at zero.

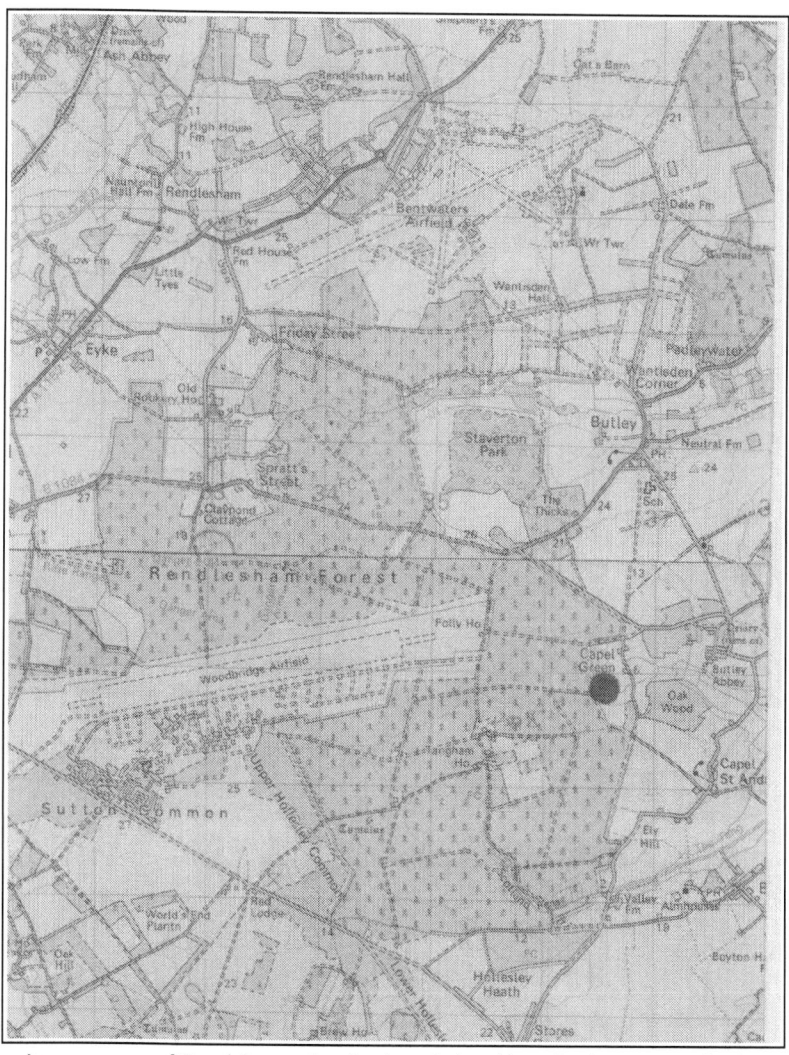

A survey map of Capel Green showing its relationship to both RAF Woodbridge and RAF Bentwaters. The red dot marks the location where the UFO appeared on the third night.

One of two photos I took on my first visit to Capel Green with Larry in February 1988. Note the slightly darkened soil at right center. This discoloration was actual and not some play of light. Also note the object in the sky to the left. Whatever it is it is not a conventional aircraft. Welcome to Suffolk East Anglia.

An almost identical view of Capel Green to the one I first experienced as Larry and I emerged from the Forest back in 1988. The incident site is about half way between this vantage point and the stand of trees at center. Note the farmhouse off to the left. Photo: Peter Robbins.

You should have a sense of just where the soil in question

Chapter 13: "Let's Talk About Soil Analysis"

came from before coming to your own conclusions about the results of the professional analysis it underwent. This is how I first experienced the location on the afternoon of 21 February 1988:

> "As the scrub pines diminished, we emerged through a grassy clearing onto a rise facing a field. When I saw the oak tree and the farmhouse, I knew we were there: Capel Green looked very much as it had been described to me.
>
> Larry's right arm shot out in an automatic gesture as we stepped onto that rise: he was pointing into the tilled field. My eyes naturally followed. "It sat right there," he said. We both got very quiet. Larry was pointing at a large, roughly circular discoloration in the earth. "Of course, that's just a coincidence..." his voice trailed off. The speed at which he'd indicated the marking in the field interested me as much as the marking itself: the man was sure that the thing he had seen that night had been sitting on that exact spot. As a researcher, I was familiar with what we call trace cases, where soil or surroundings are affected or altered as the result of a close encounter; but visible traces after eight years? Maybe it was only some play of light. We still weren't close enough to say for sure. Some conventional explanation might account for the circular shape, but its effect was positively eerie. There was nothing else like it in the field. I took a photograph and we proceeded." (*LAEG*, pages 272-273)

I ended up collecting soil samples from the darkened area and control samples from further out in the field. I used half a dozen of the plastic film canisters that held the thirty-five millimeter film I was shooting and carefully labelled them with the miniature sticky labels that came with the microcassettes I was recording on. Back at our B&B we tried mixing equal amounts of the soil with equal amounts of water. The control samples became mud very quickly. The 'affected' sample refused to reconstitute no matter how I stirred or worked it with the back of a spoon, the dirt either settling on the bottom or the jar lid or floating on the surface in a dusty film. We knew we had something but we didn't know what. When I returned to the States I contacted a laboratory that did soil analysis to look into testing the samples only to learn they needed *pounds* of it. I forwarded samples I had collected anyway with an eye on following through properly in the future.

The precise location where Larry and I observed the discoloration in the soil in February 1988 as it looked in June 1990. Photo: Peter Robbins

Sixteen months later, I returned to Suffolk pretty much on a whim following a speaking engagement in France. This time the sight in Capel Green made my jaw drop. At the precise location were the darkened area had been there was now a large roughly oval-shaped swath of green grass in an otherwise yellow field.

A fuller view of the location as it appeared in June 1990. Photo: Peter Robbins.

Chapter 13: "Let's Talk About Soil Analysis"

I was unprepared to take any samples, but was well prepared when I returned in 1992. A chemist at respected laboratory in Massachusetts had agreed to undertake a full analysis of the soil and Fedex'ed me four, two-quart heavy gage plastic containers with instructions on how to collect the samples required. The first container was to be filled with dirt from the center of the seemingly affected area, the second with soil from the 'edge,' where the normal and no-so-normal areas adjoined each other. The remaining two were to be filled with 'control' samples drawn from about one hundred and five hundred feet away from 'ground zero' which is just want I did.

An aerial photo of Caple Green, the farmhouse at top center. Photo: Paul Simpson.

Matthew Moniz was the chemist's name and he was employed by the Environmental Sciences Division of the Springborn Laboratories in Wareham, Massachusetts. I shipped the soil to him after returning home, then waited. He contacted me about two weeks later with the results. In layman's terms, this is what his analysis of the comparative samples revealed:

1. The affected samples contained in excess of four times the amount of tiny iron particles naturally occurring in soil found in

this area. When I asked Moniz what this indicated to him, he could only conclude that whatever it was that sat on that spot had exerted a tremendous electromagnetic effect on the metallic particles in the soil below and surrounding it.

2. Seed germination tests undertaken in control samples produced normal plants from seeds in expected periods of time. However identical tests conducted with affected soil samples produced only *mutations* of the plants, all of which took longer to mature than their healthy counterparts.

3, "Percent Moisture Factors of the three soil samples were taken. The two control samples close in their percentages, whereas the 'landing site soil' desiccated very rapidly and had a lower field moisture capacity than the controls."

4. "Following Percent Moisture, rehydration was attempted. The two control samples rehydrated quite easily, whereas the landing site sample required a great deal of manipulation to achieve homogeneity. The water tended to bead up and roll off the sample."

5. "Close examination under a microscope revealed no noticeable differences between the control samples, whereas the landing site sample was visibly different."

6. "The landing site sample had a higher content of silica that is indicative of exposure to high temperature or energy." In layman's terms, the sand that is naturally found in soil in this area had been reduced to silica – an interim form of glass.

> March 17, 1993
>
> Peter Robbins
> 315 West 57th Street, 20D
> New York City, NY 10019
>
> Matthew Moniz
> Springborn Laboratories, Inc.
> 790 Main Street
> Wareham, MA 02571
>
> In 1991, I had an opportunity to meet with Mr. Peter Robbins in Connecticut. He expressed a wish to have some soil samples analyzed of an alleged UFO landing site. Mr. Robbins then introduced me to his associate, Larry Warren. Mr. Warren then proceeded to tell me more about the event that he had witnessed outside of Woodbridge R.A.F.B., U.K. Mr. Robbins had made arrangements to send to me some of the soil that they had collected on their last visit to England. Upon receiving the samples, I conducted some cursory examination of the three soil samples (being LS, 50", 100") and noted the following anomolies:
>
> 1. There was visible color and texture differences between the three samples. (NOTE- This itself is not uncommon in a field, given the distance of approximately fifty feet between each sample site, but it is notable given the other anomolies involved.)
>
> 2. Percent Moisture Factors of the three soil samples were taken. The two control samples were close in their percentages, whereas the noted landing site soil dessicated very rapidly and had a lower field moisture capacity than the controls.
>
> 3. Following Percent Moisture, rehydration was attempted. The two control samples rehydrated quite easily, whereas the landing site sample required a great deal of manipulation to achieve homogenity. The water tended to bead up and roll off of the sample.
>
> 4. Close examination under a microscope revealed no noticable differences between the two control samples, whereas the landing site sample was visibly different.
>
> 5. The landing site sample had a higher content of silica that is indicative of exposure to high temperatures or energy.
>
> CONCLUSION: The conditions that the samples were stored under and the time that elapsed after the event took place is unfortunate. Yet, it is my professional opinion that these anomolies observed do warrant further investigation.

After I listened to the colonel's simplistic explanation for the changes to the soil, I felt Matt should have an opportunity to respond to them and contacted him about it. This is the email I received from Matthew Moniz on 12 August 2015 which I think will be of interest to the technically-minded in particular:

From: Moniz, Matt
To: Robbins, Peter
Sent: Wed, Aug 12, 2015 01:46 PM
Subject: Capel Green Soil Analysis

Over twenty years ago, when I was a young man and had just

entered my first laboratory job, I was asked to look at some soil purported to be from a landing site of a U.F.O. that occurred in the U.K. back in 1980. I was supplied with a few 35mm film canisters of soil that had been collected a few years before and was asked if I could see what I could find. The containers were marked control and landing site and had about half the volume full of soil in each and I had a few standard tests I thought I would try.

The normal part of my job at that point was doing testing on soil, water and other items, testing them for changing properties as related to materials that were added as potential pollutants, and how these products effected as well as broke down in these substances. This process is call degradation and Fate chemistry, and was the main form of testing required back then to determine if a new or old product was safe to be put out on the market. Having done a number of studies with a wide range of material on their effects on soil, and the guidance of a number of other scientists with years of experience, I proceeded to look at the samples provided me.

I conducted field moisture tests, mineral composition and did a small amount of chemical digestion and extraction testing. Subset samples were sent out for electron microscope testing as well. The results I obtained from these tests showed that there were notable differences in the two samples that were not like other samples I have tested. These results were seen and noted by others in my lab that were following what I was doing and had them curious as well. I made series of reports and re-conducted and confirmed my results by having another fellow scientist do as I had done.

To paraphrase what I had found back then for brevity is this:

The soil from the landing site was found to be "Hydrophobic", which means that it would not readily accept water, but would rather have it bead up and roll off, unlike the control sample.

The images of the samples under both optical as well as electron microscope showed a very strange evidence of the rounding and smoothing of the landing site soil with a noted pigment change. This, effect, the best that we were able to determine, was that the sample had been exposed to some form of heat, though not from a source such as a conventional fire. A fire would have made the individual particulates conglomerate and adhere together. There was also a much lower organic compound content as well, confirmed by using a Total Organic Carbon analyzer as well as HPLC whereas there would have been much a higher degree if ash had been poured on it as has been suggested. Now looking back with the benefit of hindsight, it appeared to be more like a high degree of frictional vibration which does generate a great deal of heat without the effect of melding and coagulation. I have seen this same effect over the years now when putting solids in an ultra sonicator, but did not relate it then. (I was young and still learning then, sorry.)

The results of the composition testing using a flame atomic absorption spectrometer showed that there was a high degree of Iron, up to 4X of the control sample, in the landing site sample. This was determined to be the cause of the reddish pigmentation. The spectrograph results of the electron microscope showed this very clearly as well. The other elements in both these samples such as Aluminum, Copper, Lead, Magnesium and Potassium and others were all within normal ranges as well as in relation to each sample soil. It was a bit of a quandary as to how the iron got into the sample though a fellow researcher made the point that if there was a high enough electromagnetic field present as well when the sample was in a semi molten state it would have bonded to the silica similar to how Pyrex is made or Borosilicate glass, or otherwise known as a form of vitrifcation.

There were larger follow up samples collected and sent to me for further testing that had anomalous results – one two-quart container of soil from the affected area, and two other two quart containers of soil taken as controls from further out in the farmers field where the event in question had occurred – not the least of which that made me wonder was the microbial tests. As a standard practice on soil the lab normally tested, we would do plate counts of bacteria colonies. The new landing site soil showed very low, almost sterile levels. This made more sense to me after the growth studies of plants I did of the landing site samples were undertaken. The control soil set of plants were regular in color and shape, while the plants grown in the landing site were discolored, with stunted growth and mild deformations. Now I had seen this before in my testing of polluted soil and knew it was an effect on the micro-fauna as there is a symbiotic relationship between them and the uptake of water and nutrients of plants, chief among these are nitrogen compounds.

A number of tests for radioactivity were performed using various forms of instrumentation. A handheld Geiger counter for one, as well as samples were volatilized and run through a Beckman scintillation counter, both of which yielded normal background radiation. It was noted that the term radiation was used in my earlier reports, though it was in normal scientific reference to states of energy, and not to be confused with particle emitting isotopes found in nuclear radiation, just to be clear for those who may misunderstand.

My ultimate hope, is that this helps to clear up any misunderstanding of what results and tests that were done in the past show. Does it prove that some craft from another planet landed in a field? By all means no. Does it show that some old farmer poured a ton of ash on a field? It shows that this does not seem to be the case at all. If you were to look at the photos of the field and the area involved, the pile would need to be very high and wide for starters, and if brush was burned on that spot, the blaze would have been seen for miles, both of which to my knowledge were not noted in the record to date.

While I can appreciate any attempt to come to grips with the results based on the limited knowledge gleaned by a close attachment to one's grandfather, the comparison is not even close. I shared the results with a fellow scientist and the remarks made about them, and we did, resulted in us having a good chuckle. I am sure that if I made comments about security procedures and practices I would receive the same reaction given the only experience I have in such matters are, my days as a bouncer in a biker bar, and animated discussions with local constabulary about the current status of the official forms and relative velocity of my personal conveyance.

With the advancement in technology we have today, I would love to revisit testing these samples again, my hope having been that some of the samples were archived. When I contacted Mr. Robbins about this, he told me he had indeed kept four of the original thirty-

Chapter 13: "Let's Talk About Soil Analysis"

five mm film canisters of soil he'd collected back in February 1988: two from the affected area, one drawn from the edge of that area, as and the other his only remaining control sample. I am pleased to know they will soon be on their way to me by mail for additional testing. Any results gleaned from such tests will not be available in time to be included in the response he is preparing, but I will make them available to him for inclusion in any future update of same. I hope this helps to clear any confusion.

Matthew Moniz

Wareham, Massachusetts

The package I sent to Matt arrived at his home a few days later. These are the first two microscope comparison photographs of the contrasting samples, both of which were collected twenty six years ago.

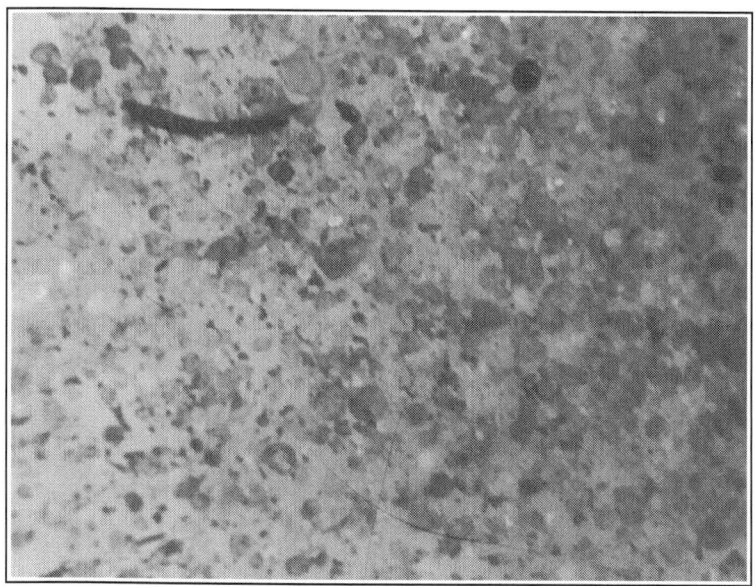

Normal (control) sample under a microscope.

Readers should understand that Moniz is not just some lab technician. His overall qualifications follow, again for the more technically-minded among us.

Matthew Moniz has worked in analytical chemistry for over 25 years. His specialty areas of research have included 8 years

155

Halt in Woodbridge

Microscope photo of sample drawn from the nearby UFO landing site.

working at environmental laboratories with a focus on soil testing, water and air quality for toxicity, as well as site contamination samples from spill events of known products and groundwater/well testing. For the past 10 years he has been involved in analytical research and development of cures for heart disease, infectious diseases and cancer. His specialty area in these fields has been in the proper use and upkeep of high end analytical instrumentation to determine the constituent components of any material and the related ratios of those components.

He is very proficient in almost every form of chemical analysis using these instruments and is now employed by the world's largest scientific manufacturer of analytical instrumentation. His current position is as a high level multi-vendor field service engineer in the Boston metro area repairing as well as installing and training end users how to operate analytical instrumentation in places like M.I.T., Harvard, Novartis institute for biomedical research, Astra Zenica, Merck, Shire, Bristol Myers Squibb, Massachusetts General hospital drug discovery labs and a number of other bio-medical and research sites located in the area.

Instrumentation he is well versed in includes HPLC- (high pressure liquid chromatography) UPLC- (Ultra high pressure Liquid chromatography) GC- (gas chromatography) Mass-Spec- (mass spectroscopy of various kinds) AA- (atomic absorption spectroscopy) ICP- (induction coupled argon plasma spectroscopy) UV-Vis- (ultraviolet and visible light spectroscopy) FTIR- (Fourier transform infrared) NMR- (nuclear magnetic resonance) scintillation detectors and a number of other analytical instrumentation. Not only does this highly trained scientist know how these complex apparatus's work and the scientific theories behind them, he is also qualified to calibrate and service and repair them.

"Let's talk about soil analysis. This is the good part."

Chapter 14:
Closing Remarks

So you can draw your own conclusions folks. He's probably going to go crazy when he hears this, but I'm tired of him putting lies out. You need to know the truth. The problem with ufology is there's too much nonsense out there. It needs scientific investigation by competent people, and not a whole lot of nonsense. That's my big frustration and that's probably one of the main reasons I'm here tonight. So…

I have to hand it to the colonel, if only for his colossal nerve. After delivering his most effective and far-reaching assault on Warren, *LAEG* and Robbins, he tells his paying audience members that he is tired of Larry "putting lies out" and that they "need to know the truth."

As the colonel says, draw your own conclusions folks.

I've got a lot more stuff, but we're gonna run out of time and I know you all have some questions and I'd be delighted to answer any reasonable question, so…are you gonna use the mic?

'Reasonable' questions only please.

I can substantiate everything I've told you tonight, and I'm going to leave some copies of everything. Now some other interesting things I can tell you while he's getting ready. I have all Budd Hopkins material, or most of it [Emphasis mine because I can't imagine what he's talking about here]. **I have all Larry Fawcett's material. All hundred, eight (?) hundred pages of it, including postcards from Larry, you**

158

name it, all the freedom of information requests and responses. I have all of it. Larry gave it all to me before he passed on a year or two ago, so I have no doubt about.

BRYANT: (asking one of the four pre-submitted questions from the audience) The next one you kind of answered. Are there any plans for everyone involved for which, I think it means for Larry, Jim, John and yourself. Any plans for you to get together round a table to try to sort out the discrepancies?

Why do I need to get together with someone who's a fraud? I mean, yeah, he's threatened to sue me, he sent me a letter that said "I'm gonna sue you if you keep it up", Sue me! Let's go to court! Let's take depositions from a whole bunch of people, I tell you, including his two ex-wives, and see what happens!

This 'cease and desist' letter from Larry Warren to Charles Halt (reproduced at the end of this chapter) dates back more than twenty years.

A few days after the colonel's talk in Woodbridge, this statement was posted on the Facebook page of Ms. Sue McAllister. Sue is a resident and native of Liverpool England. She was also married to Larry Warren. Does her statement have the weight of a legal deposition? I don't know, but it certainly bears reading:

> "I have had a few people tell me that Charles Halt made a comment about Larry Warren's ex-wives at the recent Woodbridge conference. I'd like to say I have never met the man and certainty don't want to. He knows nothing about my marriage to Larry and obviously just wants to ridicule and discredit him again. But now having to bring ex-wives into the mix he's a desperate man and a hypocrite. Take an oath and we (military) will do anything we want to you but keep your mouths shut! Do people really know what they are signing up for really? Myself and Larry's first wife are on

good terms as I am with him. Whatever happened to Larry in 1980 in Rendlesham forest deeply affected him and other air force personnel for the rest of their lives, it's called Post Traumatic Stress Disorder. Some were predisposed to the phenomena to begin with and for someone like Larry the whistle-blower, the story had to be told! He wasn't liked for it especially by Halt. Whatever has happened to Larry since, he was honourably discharged. And whatever he and other witnesses were put though after the events that changed their lives forever does not mean it did not happen to them on the third night! I'm disappointed that John Hanson and David Bryant gave Halt the opportunity to bitch so freely and say the many untrue things he did about Larry on British soil."

This is as good a place to leave off as any.

Chapter 14: Closing Remarks

```
Anthony F. Abatiell                                              James S. Abatiell
                              LAW OFFICES                             (1908-1988)
Sigismund J. Wysolmerski  ABATIELL WYSOLMERSKI & VALERIO
Also Admitted in Maryland      One Justice Square                    Paralegals
                          Merchants' Row at State Street
Matthew F. Valerio          Rutland, Vermont 05701               Lou Ann McCahey
Also Admitted in Massachusetts
                                                                 Melissa C. Stevens
                            TELEPHONE (802) 775-1508
                               FAX (802) 775-2506
```

June 22, 1995

Col. Charles I. Halt, Ret.

RE: Larry Warren, Bentwaters Incident
    Statements to EMUFORA members

Dear Mr. Halt:

    Please be advised that this office has been retained by Mr. Larry Warren to represent his personal interests regarding the incident which occurred in Rendlesham Forest on the outskirts of RAF Woodbridge, Suffolk, England during late December, 1980.

    Clearly, it is your legal prerogative to express opinions regarding the Bentwaters incident. Conversely, you have no legal right to knowingly make and publish false statements about Mr. Warren, or otherwise publicly propagate falsehoods calculated to disparage his character, credibility, or the marketability of any business projects in which Mr. Warren has an interest.

    The knowingly fallacious statements which you made in the presence of numerous EMUFORA members earlier this year regarding Mr. Warren's military record cannot be tolerated. These attempts to disparage his character and diminish his credibility, both personally and in business, must cease.

    While nobody looks forward to litigation, should these attacks continue Mr. Warren will have no choice but to pursue the legal remedies available to him to prevent further attacks.

    I thank you for your anticipated cooperation.

Very truly yours,

ABATIELL, WYSOLMERSKI & VALERIO

Matthew F. Valerio, Esq.

MFV/bfs
cc: Mr. Larry Warren

Conclusions

"I'm glad to hear that things went well. Most people's knowledge of Col. Halt comes from a few edited soundbites in various TV shows. There's no substitute for hearing unedited information and opinions 'from the horse's mouth', and getting the chance to meet such a key player up close and personal."

—Nick Pope, author, lecturer, and retired Ministry of Defence official, 12 July 2015

What drives a man to dedicate more than thirty years of his life, on and off, to the destruction of the good name and reputation of another? In this case the answer isn't simple. Then again, what drives another man to risk everything he is, has, and will be on a principle while speaking truth to power for *almost thirty-five years*? And simply because it was the right thing to do? You tell me.

On 11 July 2015 Colonel Charles I. Halt mounted his most contentious and fact-starved attack to date against Warren, *Left At East Gate,* and Robbins. To what avail? None, for anyone reading this book I hope. The speaker was smart to get the assurances he did prior to the event, especially given how he planned to utilize his final half-hour. He entered the Woodbridge Community Building fully assured that the people he did not want hearing his talk would not be hearing his talk. He knew he was free to tell his audience anything he liked that evening, then under no obligation to answer even a single question about anything he had just said. His 'right' to do so was even defended after the fact:

"He didn't badmouth anyone: he merely provided answers to the criticisms that have been levelled at him by people who cannot prove a personal involvement in the RFI. He has had to put up with crap accusing him of all kinds of bad stuff for 35 years: I think he's just about fed up with one or two people calling him names and making bucks out of something they may not even have personal experience of."

—David Bryant, author, lecturer, conference co-organizer and MC, 13 July 2015

Yes David Bryant, he did badmouth someone, and the so-called "answers" he provided amounted to absolutely nothing. If you've read this you also know that Larry Warren can "prove a personal involvement in the RFI." And as far as I'm concerned, "He has had to put up with crap accusing him of all kinds of bad stuff for 35 years: I think he's just about fed up with one or two people calling him names and making bucks out of something they may not even have personal experience of."

> "Charles Halt exercised his democratic right to say what he wanted to say in the same way that you have yourself made your comments available on the Internet – democracy at work. ..."
>
> —John Hanson, Publisher, author and conference organizer, responding to a criticism from a Halt talk audience member, 14 July 2015

John Hanson, it is no one's "democratic right" to represent fiction as fact if their intent is to deceive and they are charging others twenty pounds each to hear it. I don't think this was your intent but it was Mr. Halt's. In inviting him to speak, covering his expenses, securing the venue and promoting the event, you and David facilitated his slander. He made his comments, not only in front of an audience, but also in the full knowledge he was being filmed by an authorized cameraman, and that the film would inevitably find its way into circulation. The same can be said of his accompanying regional BBC Radio interview.

The colonel made many references to *Left At East Gate* in his talk, even to exact page numbers, so he has clearly read it thoroughly. In which case, any factual evidence that he has contradicted would also constitute slander/defamation of character, because he uttered it with clear knowledge of the facts before him and otherwise available to him.

This is as good a time as any to introduce some possible extenuating circumstances, none of which I believe to be to be

Halt in Woodbridge

the case. Still, if any are factual they could help to explain the colonel's obsessive behavior toward Larry, and in a manner that might relieve him of responsibility for his actions. These questions are asked intending no lack of respect. They just need to be asked.

Charles Halt looks and sounds to be in good health in his recent video appearances. I hope he is. On 11 July he looked much in his element, at home in both lecture hall and forest and deliberate in his words and actions at both locations. But, is there any possibility that his seemingly-illogical decision to tell his audience nothing but untruths for half an hour might in itself be some kind of symptom, presenting sign or indication of an organic medical problem, memory disorder, or worse? Further, is there any possibility that Charles's long obsession has somehow turned into a diagnosable psychological disorder? A layman's opinion? I don't think, hope or believe these circumstances apply and wish Charles only good health.

On his 11 July walk in the forest the colonel said he thought I wasn't dumb. Let me say for the record that I think Charles Halt is smart. Smart enough that I strongly doubt the number and variety of untruths he 'shared' with his audience could possibly be accounted for by extreme carelessness, a wild series of unhappy coincidences, simple stupidity or incredibly poor investigative skills. There was a pattern in the accusations though, and one I was familiar with. In fact I'd written about another such attempt to undermine Larry Warren and *Left At East Gate* only last year:

> "Create/invent some new 'details' and attribute them to Warren, even though they bear no resemblance to anything he has ever said or written. Base all of your accusations, observations and conclusions relating to Larry Warren and to his co-author's research on incomplete and convoluted data, always 'borrowed' from their own book. ... Consistently and erroneously conclude that Larry Warren is the single source of certain information while ignoring all evidence presented in *Left At East Gate* which repeatedly establishes the contrary to be true." (*Deliberate Deception* 2015).

Conclusions

I don't think or believe any extenuating circumstances apply here either. But I do think Charles Halt may have been given assistance in putting together the 'exhibits' for his assault in Woodbridge. Maybe it's just some lug-nut part of the military/intelligence mindset, but there is something so obtusely-executed about this series of 'Warren is wrong Halt is right' charges that I can see it being the handiwork of not-that-knowledgeable (about the RFI) Pentagon staffers. Then again they could have all be a reflection of Halt's thinking alone, or a combination of both. And if he were somehow shown up for his many twistings of the truth there would be nothing to connect him with higher-ups. Indeed, if those above him were to have told the colonel he should include a bunch of 'pre-researched' Warren and *LAEG* sure-to-destroy material, would he actually have bothered to look them all up or just added them to the ones he was already at work on?

An additional thought before leaving off. Repeated references to my 'very good friend,' 'a buddy of mine,' 'we hung out together,' 'I have the information,' 'take my word for it,' and the occasional 'trust me' (I'm a colonel) permeate Mr. Halt's talk. Is this the way he routinely employs language when speaking before an audience? Are these simply unconscious catch-phrases informed by a career in the assertive world of military culture? Were they random figures of speech or well-chosen phrases calculated to reinforce his presence as a knowledgeable figure?

Then again, they might represent entry level Neuro-linguistic programming. Paraphrasing Wikipedia,' NLP is an approach to communication, personal development, and psychotherapy. It puts forward that connections between the neurological processes and behavioral patterns learned through experience ("programming") can be changed to achieve specific goals in life.' It can also be used to make somebody buy something. Or be more forceful and successful at a business meeting. Or sway and impress an audience full of people. This especially so when not a shred of evidence is presented. I don't think this is such a wild possibility

The colonel had wanted our book 'to get things right.' He first made that clear to us years before it was published. We did get things right, to the greatest degree we were able at the time. Just not from his perspective. Personally I think we got too much right for his perspective. That's why there are parts of *Left At East Gate* he would rather you not read. But is there anything *about him* in the book that he might have taken objection to?

Charles I. Halt's name appears more than fifty times in the index of *LAEG*. Read through them and you'll see not a one is mean-spirited, mocking, or in any other way disrespectful. There was that single criticism I made at the end of our book, but otherwise, nothing. When *Left At East Gate* was republished on the twenty-fifth anniversary of the RFI I didn't add a word to what I'd already written about the colonel. Larry did add two statements. Were they in any way provocative? You be the judge:

> "I had not been to Washington since 1992, when we had interviewed Charles Halt. It was a shame that Halt would not be joining us at the National Press Club, though I hoped he would." (*On the first Disclosure event held at the National Press Club in May 2001, LAEG,* page xv)

> "Charles Halt confirmed that others and I were messed with after the incidents. Halt, I must say, should be proud of himself for what he said on the show. No one of his rank had gone so far as he did on that documentary. In my opinion the man is a hero, and I salute him." (*LAEG,* page xx)

"In my opinion the man is a hero, and I salute him." The show Larry refers to is the Sci-Fi Channel's feature-length *Invasion In the Rendlesham Forest*, first broadcast in 2005. I'm proud to have submitted the original proposal for this documentary to the network's Director of Special Projects. Larry and I also gave him contact information for Col. Halt, John, Burroughs, Jim Penniston and other witnesses. When contacted by the project director the first thing the colonel wanted to know was if Warren and Robbins were involved. Because if so, he would not be. 'Who would you rather have? A colonel or an airman' was his basic refrain. The

Project Director refused to agree to his term and Charles acquiesced. He would not however agree to appear on camera with us which was something we could live with. I always tried to keep things respectful toward Mr. Halt, only coming back at him on those occasions he'd initiate another of his attacks. Otherwise take the high road and show respect. Do I still believe the things I did about Halt in 1996? Some of them. This is what I wrote about him that year:

"Charles I. Halt was an Air Force career officer serving his country with distinction. Being identified as the highest ranking officer to witness any of the events, as well as the author of what is still the only authentic document to surface on them, was undoubtedly the worst thing that ever happened to this officer's military career. By 1991, when he retired as a full colonel, Charles Halt had taken more Bentwaters heat than any other officer in the Air Force. It is my belief that during the incidents themselves, in their aftermath, and ever since, he has continued to serve the Air Force with more distinction than any of us will ever be able to ascertain. I respect Mr. Halt, admire his sense of loyalty, and only wish him the best in life. ...."

On my best behavior here but it didn't last long:

"—however, I cannot and will not condone certain things he has said about my co-author: they're just not correct. Let me backtrack.

As I understood it, the Air Force documents Mr. Halt had referred to in our phone conversations came to him via a Pentagon contact. It is clear in the transcripts that he had no doubts about their validity, and if Larry and I could get down to meet him, he would show them to us.

We had been looking forward to seeing those papers, but we never did. I think the reason was that at some point during our talk, perhaps after reading through some of Larry's service record, Mr. Halt realized there was a problem with his own papers. My feeling is that they were Pentagon generated disinformation, designed to make Charles Halt believe that Larry Warren could not have been posted to D Flight, or any other flight on the night in question, thus reinforcing his belief that Warren was a liar. I'm not sure what Larry or Bob made of it at the time, but the impression was real enough for me that I chose not to press the issue.

I am convinced that the lion's share of information that Mr. Halt did share with us was the truth as he knew it, or suspected it to be. Some key points of what he told us are worth reviewing. More than one thing happened. The real story was what happened afterward, "not what happened there." Afterward was more important than the night before. Larry had been "meddled with", but it was not an experiment. Bentwaters Security Police Logs and blotter for the nights in question had disappeared. Larry and I had no clear idea of what we had gotten ourselves into, or how deep in it we were. We should assume our phone lines were dirty, and be as concerned about our health and well-being as he was about his.

He told us several other things I would have liked to publish, but not before asking me to turn off the recorder. I complied with each request. Although he did not say, "I am telling you this in confidence," that was what I understood him to mean.

In July of 1994, Charles Halt returned to England and addressed a UFO conference in Manchester. Sometime during that weekend, he was speaking informally with a group of audience members when one of them asked a question about Larry Warren. Larry had not been there, came the answer. His account was untrue. If anything was not true here, it was the Colonel's answer.

Two years earlier, Charles Halt said to Larry Warren: "I think you sincerely believe what you're saying and you may be right, and I can't say you're lying, but I find flaws here and there that I have to have them resolved for myself."

Yes, it is true; maybe Larry only believed what he was saying, and that was the extent of it. And yes, I have felt the same compunction he has; to find the flaws and resolve them. But the fact is that Charles Halt knows what Larry is saying may be correct. Mr. Halt knew that in June of 1992. It was still true two years later.

I never served in the military, but have grown to appreciate the code that many who have live by. I think that Charles Halt, like many retired career officers, continues to adhere to the standards of that code in civilian life. In context, I can only commend him for it. But I live by a code too, and Charles Halt broke it when he answered that question in Manchester. We know he made the remarks because a researcher friend of ours asked the question. No, we hadn't asked him to. There were also two other people in the group who'd heard Larry and me several months earlier in Nottingham. The pair never spoke with our researcher friend, but all got into contact with us with the same news shortly after. For me, Charles Halt's response was the equivalent of breaking a confidence. That is why I have decided to break the confidence that was implied when Charles Halt asked me to turn off my tape recorder. He told us three things. He was very much aware of the NSA's interest in Larry. He had personally attempted to gain access to Larry's military record, without success. Light beams [from the unknowns] had penetrated the hardened bunkers of Bentwaters. That was it, and that is plenty.

I hope Charles Halt understands why I have taken this action. My co-author wanted to do it himself, but his doing so might have appeared personally based. This is not a personal matter." (*LAEG*, pages 411-413)

And so it remains. Not a personal matter today any more than it was in 1996. I think the colonel did take it personally though. In 2007 Robert Hastings, author of *UFOs and Nukes*, interviewed Mr. Halt for his 2008 book and, in Hastings' and Halt's words:

"Following the telephone interview, Halt expanded upon these remarks via email. He wrote, "I never told [*Left At East Gate* author] Peter Robbins any structure was penetrated by beams. I was several miles away. From my view, a beam or more came down near the WSA I don't know for a fact that the beams landed there. I know they were in the area. I was too far away but relied on the radio chatter which indicated the beams landed there. The objects in the sky came from the east and moved west, skirting Woodbridge and approaching Bentwaters. When beams came down, the objects were closer to the Bentwaters WSA – just to the north of the facility. Only one object came overhead and briefly sent down a beam at our feet. The other three objects stayed just west of us. And one or more of them sent down the beams to the WSA. They were far enough away that we couldn't tell which one or how many sent down beams. We could see several beams and members in the

WSA went on the radio to report them. I don't remember any names at this point." (*UFOs and Nukes,* pages 396-397)

Right. In 1993 Charles Halt told us that beams from the unknowns had somehow penetrated structures in the WSA. I was sitting across the table from him when he said it. Nothing in his statement to Robert Hastings changes that in the least.

We now come to the question—has Charles Halt been 'leaned on,' or ordered, or requested, or otherwise encouraged and/or assisted in his campaign against the RFI whistle-blower? If so, we can only wonder if it began immediately following the events of December 1980 or sometime after that. I doubt the colonel will ever tell us. For myself, I've little doubt he has been influenced, at least to some degree over the years. I'm equally certain he would go after Larry with no encouragement or assistance necessary. So are a good number of thinking people who've posted their thoughts on this in appropriate Facebook threads. Here are three from Facebook friends in the UK whose names I neglected to note. With apologies guys:

"Halt is being instructed to continuously slander Larry by his controllers because throughout the past 34 years Larry Warren had consistently identified himself by his words and actions as the biggest and most troublesome leak in the matter of the RFI."

"The very fact that Halt continues to try to ridicule/slander you in various ways should ring alarm bells with most people (or at least anyone with their head screwed on). It's obvious he has an ongoing agenda to reduce the public's trust in you and your version of events, which in my eyes indicates that it is what took place."

"Throw enough mud around and some will stick. Halt has a pension to protect, and seems to be someone's attack dog, now he just seems to be used as a tool to discredit Larry. I don't think Halt necessarily even believes things that he says. The powers that be may be hoping one day Larry will just get fed up with the assaults and just walk away."

All solid, logical observations to me. What would be surprising to learn was that pressured had *not* been applied over the years. Whatever else I can tell you, Charles had been

Conclusions

thinking about giving this particular talk for decades. In February 1993 he told Larry, me, and Bob Oeschsler, "I intend someday to have my day in court in England, publicly, if I have the opportunity. I'd like to state for the record what I saw and they'll be some people that are very embarrassed." (Charles Halt, *LAEG* pages 362)

Were Larry and I the people he had in mind to embarrass at some future date or just among the contenders? Had our book come our 'right' for Charles I expect other heads would have been on the chopping block that summer's day in Woodbridge. However I do agree that this man should have his day in court in England. I just think it should held as an event separate from his 11 July talk.

The colonel essentially ended his talk with this response to the one Warren-related question taken:

Why do I need to get together with someone who's a fraud? I mean, yeah, he's threatened to sue me, he sent me a letter that said "I'm gonna sue you if you keep it up", Sue me! Let's go to court! Let's take depositions from a whole bunch of people, I tell you, including his two ex-wives, and see what happens!

"Sue me! Let's go to court! Let's take depositions...." "I intend someday to have my day in court in England..." I say let Charles Halt have that day in court, in England, but a real English courtroom.

Have you ever heard a man so enthusiastic over the possibility of having a lawsuit filed against him? This of course is a decision that Larry Warren will have to make. Even when your evidence is overwhelming, mounting such a legal action can be costly and time consuming. And in the event of a decision for Warren, collecting damages from someone living in another country could prove to be a challenge in itself, not that money is the issue here.

For anyone unaware, Larry has been a resident of Liverpool England since 2000 and thus whose rights are protected under English as well as American law. I'm not a lawyer and did not choose to consult one while preparing this response. This is my personal opinion and nothing more. But it's an opinion informed by something of a crash course these past weeks on the statutes, arguments and penalties regarding the charges of slander and libel under English law. I had help from a friend who used to work at a law office in the UK. Here's the highly compressed version with a few URLs for those who may wish to press deeper.

- In the UK, there is no statutory definition of defamation. Instead, various statements by the courts contribute to a common law definition of defamation.
- What are the elements necessary for a charge of libel or slander to be leveled? The elements of a defamation suit, whether slander or libel, are:

  1. A defamatory statement

  2. Published to a third party

  3. Which the speaker knew or should have known was false

  4. That causes injury to the subject of the communication

- In the noun form: oral defamation, in which someone tells one or more persons an untruth about another which untruth will harm the reputation of the person defamed. Slander is a civil wrong (tort) and can be the basis for a lawsuit. Damages (payoff for worth) for slander may be limited to actual (special) damages unless there is malicious intent, since such damages are usually difficult to specify and harder to prove.
- English law allows actions for libel to be brought in the High Court for any published statements which are alleged to defame a named or identifiable individual(s) (under English law companies are legal persons, and may bring suit for defamation) in a manner which causes them loss in their trade

or profession, or causes a reasonable person to think worse of him, her or them

- Such a judgement could result in a one or two-year jail sentence. The norm is a (large) fine for damages caused. If Charles Halt were to ever write a book that repeated known untruths about Larry or me or our book it could allow for an additional action to be taken against him for both slander and libel.[7]

The defamation Halt has inflicted on Warren has been extremely long-term, particularly malicious, patently untrue, and psychologically harmful. It could lead to higher fines if proven in court:[8]

Where does this leave us? With a small handful of questions and a few remaining thoughts and opinions. My first question is, how do the people who attended the colonel's talk feel about all this? It was they who paid their money in good faith to hear a talk by an allegedly-respected figure in an important event they had a genuine interest in. In turn they were lied to, misled and misinformed throughout the final portion of the program. I think they all deserve to receive sincere, written apologies from the speaker and from the organizers. I also think that those who wish should receive their money back. I think John Hanson and David Bryant should take whatever actions necessary to recover whatever monies they are able from Mr. Halt. If that means initiating their own legal action him then so be it. I also feel that Mr. Halt owes a separate apology to all the men who served under him during the RFI and who he came to find fault with in its aftermath.

But here John Hanson and David Bryant are only the latest in a line of people owing Larry Warren an apology. If I were Hanson and Bryant I would consider making their apologies as

---

[7] http://www.inbrief.co.uk/offences/crime-of-defamatory-libel.htm

[8] https://www.lawontheweb.co.uk/legal-help/definition-of-defamatory and http://www.hse.gov.uk/enforce/enforcementguide/court/reporting-defamation.htm

Halt in Woodbridge

public to Larry as possible. Otherwise, if they are men of faith, they may want to pray that he does not take them to court though he would be very much within his rights to do so. Both the organizers acted to facilitate and protect the slanderer even if unknowingly in certain respects. And I expect Larry might stand a far better chance of collecting on a fully-domestic verdict in his favor than he would against Charles Halt. Hanson and Bryant should also consider separating themselves from the colonel, and if they have come to realize they were lied to and believed Charles's nonsense they should say so.

To the armchair researchers and keyboard warriors who have for decades expressed their negative views and opinions towards the 'believability' of Larry Warren's account versus the seemingly better grounded account and views of Col. Halt, it's time to update your databases and show some respect for someone who really stands for something.

I'll say the same to the members of the UFO research community. Col. Halt is not a fully honest participant in this so-called dialogue. His only real goal and intention has to mislead and disinform, primarily with regard to the credibility of this key witness. And do not confuse what has been going on here with a 'difference of opinion.' Neither is it an example of the 'the kind of infighting that makes us all look bad.' Would *you* ever insist certain people be barred at the door should they try to attend one of your talks? Would you ever refuse to answer any audience questions about a talk you had just given? Would you, for any reason, ever use part of your lecture time to intentionally and knowingly tell an audience one absolute untruth after another because it fit your agenda? No? Then you should consider actually taking a public position on this, even if the overwhelming likelihood is that Larry Warren is not a fan of yours. The reason is simple. So many of us in the UFO research community have let this witness/whistle-blower down so often for so many years.

With the thirty-fifth anniversary of the Rendlesham Forest

incident fast approaching this is what I would most like to see happen. It would involve as many of the RFI witnesses who were comfortable doing so, including the best-known as well as relatively or completely unknown, to us anyway. Let them get away for a long weekend together, Woodbridge being the ideal location. Let them spend their days together in any way they wish. Being there for and with each other, talking about whatever they wish. No researchers, investigators, writers, authorities, media folk or personalities. Just them. And when they emerge from their time together, then maybe hold a conference and share some of what they'd learned with their audience. I think John Burroughs is the person with the best credentials to make this happen and I know he'll have the support of every person who really cares about this subject.

What does this all come down to for me? Having done my best to sort out what's true from what's not as best I've been able. Hoping that others will acknowledge the facts established here. Doing something because it was the right thing to do. Never forgetting what drives me in the Rendlesham Forest incident. Charles Halt or no Charles Halt:

> "...I felt the return of an old, familiar feeling, one I first encountered in association with the Rendlesham incident sometime during the second half of 1988. It was pure, unadulterated anger, the specific source of which was rooted in my growing realization of how truly awful Larry Warren had been treated by the service branch he'd sworn to serve. As Larry and I continued to work together over the years, I read and studied everything relevant I could get my hands on. At the same time our shared obsession repeatedly drove us back to Suffolk where we continued our research, interviews, and visits to relevant locations. My anger grew to encompass a deeper appreciation for the RFI's impact on the lives of others who had been involved. It was this and not my interest in UFOs per se, that became the driving force that compelled me, (obsessively at times, ..), to work this case, week after week, month after month and year after year for almost a decade, this in an effort to answer Larry's and my own questions about Rendlesham, and to complete the book in as professional a manner as possible. And for several pages

of this final chapter I could not help thinking about Larry's story, and reflected in my mind's eye, the stories that lay with Jim and John, Ed Cabansac, Adrian Bustinza, Bobby Ball, Bruce Englund, Bonnie Tamplin, Ray Gulyas, Steve LaPlume, Steve Longero, Greg Battram, and so many others, the great majority of whom I would never meet, not forgetting the story of a young airman who roomed for a while with my friend at RAF Bentwaters and went by a Southern nickname, then was no more." (*Deliberate Deception*, 2014)

Larry Warren and Peter Robbins, RAF Bentwaters flight line, 28 December 2010. Photo: Ronnie Dugdale.

Final words? Remember that the person who set all this in motion was not the tough guy in the above photo. That person was still a teenager when he made the decision to go up against the forces that be and damn the consequences. A lot for a nineteen-year old to take on. And it cost him. That's the face to remember.

Conclusions

Larry Warren in his dorm room shortly after the incident, Eagles poster in background. 1981.

This is how Larry concluded his final chapter in *Left At East Gate*:

> "...in a farmer's field that borders a large forest on the eastern coast of England, I will always be able to pick up a handful of my deepest fears, hold it a moment, then let it go. In this place, I will always be nineteen years old." (*LAEG*, page 399)

That's how I'll conclude as well.

Capel Green February 2014. Photo: Peter Robbins.

177

About the Author

Peter Robbins is an investigative writer specializing in the subject of UFOs. He has more that thirty-five years' experience as a writer, researcher, investigator, lecturer, and author. A regular fixture on radio shows in the US and UK, he has appeared as a guest on and been consultant to numerous TV programs and documentaries. Robbins has spoken on UFOs, Dr. Wilhelm Reich, and related subjects at local, regional, national, and international conferences as well as for schools, universities, libraries, and organizations. He is co-author (along with Larry Warren) of the British best-seller *Left at East Gate: A First-Hand Account of the Rendlesham Forest UFO Incident, Its Cover-Up and Investigation*. He is the author of *Deliberate Deception: A Case of Disinformation in the UFO Research Community*, and *Halt In Woodbridge: An Air Force Colonel's Thirty-Year Fight To Silence An Authentic UFO Whistle-Blower*.

Printed in Great Britain
by Amazon.co.uk, Ltd.,
Marston Gate.